My Parent My Turn

At some point, 'honoring your father and mother' may mean caring for them as they once cared for you

MY PARENT MY TURN

Harris McIlwain, M.D.
& Debra Bruce

BROADMAN
& HOLMAN
PUBLISHERS

Nashville, Tennessee

4261-79

0-8054-6179-5

Dewey Decimal Classification: 362.6

Subject Heading: Elderly—Home Care \ Parent and Child \ Aging Parents

Library of Congress Card Catalog Number: 94-45744

Unless noted otherwise, Scripture quotations are from the Bible in Today's English Version, Old Testament copyright © American Bible Society 1976; New Testament copyright © American Bible Society 1966, 1971, 1976, used by permission. Verses marked TLB are from The Living Bible, copyright © Tyndale House Publishers, Wheaton, Ill., 1971, used by permission.

Page Design by Trina Hollister

Library of Congress Cataloging-in-Publication Data

McIlwain, Harris H.

My parent, my turn / Harris H. McIlwain, Debra Fulghum Bruce.

p. cm.

Includes bibliographical references.

ISBN 0-8054-6179-5

1. Aged—Care—United States. 2. Aging parents—Care—United States.

I. Bruce, Debra Fulghum, 1951– . II. Title.

HV1461.M383   1995

362.6'0973—dc20

94-45744

CIP

1 2 3 4 5 99 98 97 96 95

We dedicate this book to Linda McIlwain.
This book began as her dream to help caregivers and their families.

"Little children, let us stop just saying we love
people; let us really love them, and show
it by our actions."
1 John 3:18, TLB

ACKNOWLEDGMENTS

We are deeply grateful to the many people who assisted with this guide for caregivers:

TO OUR FAMILIES:

Linda McIlwain, for the hundreds of hours of research and consultation as she shared her expertise as a senior advocate and her practical ideas in coping with caregiving problems;

Bob Bruce, for the long hours of spiritual counsel and for sharing his years of experience in working with senior adults in the local church;

Laura and Kim McIlwain, for the months spent researching exercise and activity and for their commitment to sensitivity and respect for senior adults;

Rob and Brittnye Bruce, for spending numerous long summer days at the library reviewing microfilm, making copies, proofreading material, and preparing family meals as deadlines approached;

Ashley Bruce and Mike, Ginah, and Danny McIlwain, for sometimes having to spend quality time instead of quantity time with their parents while we wrote this book;

Roy Fulghum, for making time to give in-depth financial information and retirement guidance;

Jewel Fulghum and Cordelia McIlwain, for the wonderment of their ongoing patience and loving advice;

Lori Steinmeyer, M.S., R.D./L.D., for her timely material on nutrition for the elderly; and

Mac Steinmeyer, for his masterful computing skills.

TO OUR FRIENDS:

Angus Williams Jr., senior agent, Principal Financial Group, Tampa, Florida, for giving a greater understanding of insurance for retirement years;

James A. Wessman, CPA, senior partner, Thomas Craig & Company, Tampa, Florida, for up-to-date investment and financial information;

Ginah Butler, for the precious time she gave in consultation as well as many innovative ideas on how to make this book practical for all caregivers;

Caroline C. Jones, for her inspiration to other seniors as she truly lives her devout faith in God and enjoys every moment of His creation;

Elizabeth Owens Haseman, Ph.D., CCC, for her knowledge and expertise in speech and language pathology;

Trudy Pascucci, publisher of *Living Well Today*, for permission to reprint information regarding the elderly; and

Janis Whipple, our steadfast and vivacious editor, who believed in the merit and timeliness of this manuscript.

CONTENTS

INTRODUCTION:
THE CAREGIVING CRISIS

"Just when things were going so well," Emily (not her real name), a forty-four-year-old school teacher and mother of three, told us after her seventy-four-year-old father fractured his hip for the second time in two years. "Dad had just gotten his strength back from the first hip ordeal, and he was so happy to move back into his apartment, and then this happens. Mom's gone, and he's so alone. What is he going to do now?"

Emily looked up with tears in her eyes and asked, "What are we going to do now?"

John, a thirty-nine-year-old attorney and father of two, voiced a similar concern. "I was packing the car to take my boys camping last Friday afternoon when the phone rang. It was my mother's next door neighbor who said that Mom hadn't answered her phone or door all day. What am I going to do? Mom is pretty healthy, but now since Dad died, she lives alone—four hundred miles away. I worry all the time that she will fall or get sick, and no one will ever know."

Vicki tells of an all too common problem with her eighty-five-year old mother. "Mom can't live alone anymore since her diabetes worsened, but she doesn't want to live with us either. She claims the kids and their friends make her nervous. She also doesn't want to go to a nursing home; she is much too active for that. What do I do? Who will take care of her?"

For some families, a parent's minor fall or illness is insignificant. But for many families, repeated illness or other regression means that it is time to take control—to do something immediate before a major crisis occurs.

CONSIDER THE FACTS

The proportion of our population in the mature years is larger than ever before; every ninth American is age sixty-five or older. In 1900, there were 3 million people sixty-five and older in the United States (about 4 percent of the total United States population). In 1991, this figure increased to approximately 31.8 million Americans. By the year 2020, the Census Bureau projects that there will be more than 70 million Americans aged fifty-five and older (over 20 percent of all Americans). Older adults are America's largest minority group, and America has more older adults than the entire population of Canada.

The statistics are startling: At least 4.4 million noninstitutionalized (persons living at home) Americans over age sixty-five have disabilities or chronic physical impairments that limit their daily activities. About 32 percent of them—overwhelmingly male—live with spouses who provide care; another 35 percent live with other relatives or nonrelatives—usually their children.

Until the late seventies, the only available choice for elderly Americans who no longer could care for themselves was to go to a nursing home, or, if necessary, move in with one of their adult children and family. But the added stresses on families when aging parents move in can become overbearing—if not handled properly. The family unit that once focused on raising children becomes focused on caring for grandparents, leaving strained family relations, children who miss a part of their childhood, and often resentment from the caregivers.

Nursing home costs have skyrocketed to the point where quality residential care is prohibitive to most Americans. The average cost for nursing home care is now more than $30,000 per year—and this represents merely basic care.

WHO WILL TAKE CARE OF OUR PARENTS?

So, the question remains: Who will take care of our parents? A recent congressional study showed that American women will spend seventeen years raising children and eighteen years caring for their parents. Add to this caregiving challenge the millions of American women who must also work outside the home, either full or part time, and then take care of dependent children and parents after hours.

This book will help you understand how to effectively care for loved ones in this life stage—a stage that many may want to ignore, but one that most of us will be faced with sooner or later. We will provide you with insight and alternative caregiving opportunities for the nineties. And we will discuss all aspects of aging, including health problems, physical symptoms, nutritional needs, emotional changes, financial planning, and spiritual needs. We feel that all of these factors contribute to the overall health and well-being of the mature adult.

END CATASTROPHIES

The number of elderly that have support from their children is most significant. Some studies report that four out of five older persons have living children and 66 percent of these persons live within thirty minutes of one of their children. As many as 62 percent have weekly visits with their children, and as many as 76 percent have weekly phone calls. These figures show that the potential for assistance and problem solving are great. Under the best of circumstances, this assistance from child to parent may be only a phone call and home visit once or twice a week, as well as availability for support when a crisis such as illness, financial problems, or even death occurs.

No matter how close assistance is for the elderly, numerous potentials for hazards occur each day. Did you know that one out of nine noninstitutionalized Americans (again, those living at home) ages sixty-five to seventy-four has difficulty with household chores, meal preparation, financial matters, and transportation? The numbers are greater as age increases, with some reports of one in four in the seventy-five to eighty-four age group having difficulty and three out of every five people in the eighty-five and older age group having difficulty caring for themselves.

As many as 40 percent of individuals sixty-five and older have nutrition-related health problems. These individuals do not have the benefit of care at home unless they are covered by comprehensive (and often expensive) supplemental insurance policies, have plenty of money to hire someone to assist them with daily living tasks, have family and friends to care for them, or meet the criteria for Medicaid services and are not on a long waiting list. These people are in crisis if they cannot cover these services in some manner.

The real concern is how to take care of everyday problems—before a catastrophe occurs. Especially if you are a child living away from your aging parents, the following questions are pressing realities for you:

- How will Mom and Dad get to the store for groceries or to the doctor for appointments?

- Who will take them to church each week if they are unable to drive?

- What steps can be taken to prevent accidents and make their home safe?

- Who will make meals when they are are ill?

- Who will help with repairs when they are unable to care for their home?

- Who will care for them after surgery?

- Who will make sure they follow the doctor's orders, take prescriptions, and stay on their diet?

- Who will check their financial status periodically, making sure social security payments are received, bills are paid, and accounts are in order?

- Who will bathe them each day if they are unable to do this on their own?

- Who will take care of the lawn and their property?

- How should we determine when they should stop driving?

- Who will maintain their car and their appliances?

- What about home security? Who will help protect our parents?

There are so many more.

My Parent, My Turn is your handbook for caregiving. We will teach you ways to problem solve—ahead of time—so that tragedies are less likely to occur with your aging loved one. Common problems that may occur as your parents age are discussed, and practical, tried-and-true solutions are given that will create the least amount of negative disruption to you and your family. Your relationship as child/caregiver can remain strong if problems are prevented ahead of time rather than waiting for intervention during crisis.

"I am so glad that we helped Dad get a boarder this year," Sidney said regarding his seventy-year-old single father. "When we were visiting him at Christmastime, we noticed a pot of boiling water on the stove. Dad did not even remember putting it there!"

"Now that he has another gentleman living with him, we feel relief knowing they can watch out for each other. We still call each day and visit twice a week, but we are not as worried about Dad's forgetfulness."

Another caregiver, Virginia, tells of having home care for her mother three times a week. "Living several hours away, I need to make sure that Mother is eating well, that her home is clean, and that she takes her medications. She is still so active in her church and even assists with teaching the preschool Sunday School class, but I just need this extra assurance that her personal needs are being met."

Pat, a secretary and single mother of twin teenage girls, tells of enrolling her parents in a program at their church. "I have to work as the only source of income for our family. So when Mom and Dad became less active at home and began to sit around and watch television all day, I called our church to see if there were any programs.

"Our pastor told me about an adult day care program that had just started. This provides a hot lunch, activities, and even field trips each week. It was perfect for my parents! For a nominal charge, the church van picks them up each morning and takes them home at night. I then go over and fix their dinner. They are more alert and healthier than they have been in years!"

Problems with the aged have the potential to be life-threatening and catastrophic—or they can be seen as stepping stones into a fuller, more productive life for seniors and satisfaction for the caregiver.

There Is Good News!

The good news is that you can learn to prevent problems that cause family stress as you care for aging parents. By becoming aware of "signals" that let you know a problem is about to occur, you can take control of the situation before it becomes explosive. This will not be easy, but the caregiving style discussed in this book is manageable, allowing you to feel in control rather than living with constant anxiety over "what might happen next." Just as it is wise to take classes on parenting when children are born, it is equally important to educate yourself in how to be a quality, loving caregiver. This book will provide this education for you.

The Christian's Challenge

The purpose of this book is not only to instruct you in the fundamentals of caring for an aging parent, it is also about challenge—the tremendous challenge we have as Christians to minister in our neighborhoods and communities to the aged. In the midst of personal concern over aging parents, there still remains an astounding number of elderly adults in the United States who do not have any family. In fact, 24 percent of the senior population must depend on friends, neighbors, and the church for support. This may be one of the most pathetic situations in our society—the "frail" elderly without family, who spend their last years alone, unloved, and without adequate medical and emotional care.

The oldest group of Americans today are women; 67 percent of those eighty-five and older are females. Of this group, a staggering 58 percent live alone! This situation defines itself as a mission for every church. The latest reports indicate that as many as 8 million Americans today need assistance with personal care. The challenge to Christians today is to reach out with Christ's love and touch these lives.

DESIGN A PLAN OF ACTION

This book will enable you to design a plan of action as you care for aging parents and the elderly in your church or community. We have tried to make this an easy-to-read and practical guide with suggestions that can be used immediately. In this book we share our years of experiences and the wisdom that other professionals have taught us. Rather than expound on the theories behind caregiving and aging, we will teach you how to develop a mind-set for balance in your life and how to take some important steps to achieve this.

Because of the vast improvement in health care over the past ninety years, including more prevention and treatment of diseases, the average life span has increased greatly. And due to this longer life span, many people are concerned about the quality of these extra years. Most of us do not look forward to added years of life as unhappy, sick, or lonely older adults, nor do we wish this for our parents. Simply adding years to a person's life is no longer acceptable to anyone. The goal as Christian children should be to help make those extra years as enjoyable, fulfilling, and productive as possible for our parents and for all people.

After all, of what purpose is our faith unless it is given away? Good intentions to help others are admirable, but unless action takes place, they truly have no meaning. It has been said that "we make a living by what we get out of life, but we make a life by what we give." Putting feet to our Christian faith through balanced caregiving enables us to add fulfillment to our life and to the lives of others.

First John 3:18 offers us a challenge to begin a lifestyle of good intentions and deeds as we balance caregiving with raising our families: "Little children, let us stop just saying we love people; let us really love them, and show it by our action."

Today you may be your parent's child, but you are also just starting a life-changing journey to learn how to be a nurturing caregiver to your parent. In this book you will encounter some very real situations along with a world of practical and professional advice to put "feet to faith" and demonstrate to those cherished senior adults in your life the real meaning of agape, or Christlike, love.

The challenge to care for all God's people is ours!

1

PREVENTION AND PLANNING: THE KEYS TO BALANCE

Welcome to the unpredictable but rewarding world of caregiving. Studies show that most young and middle-age adults today now face new roles. Not only are millions caring for dependent children, but soon they must care for aging parents. As most caregivers testify, these years can be the most rewarding time in your life, or they can be filled with anxiety, depression, and bitterness—depending on how you and your parents plan for health and safety while preventing illness and mishaps.

As the adult child, you will now be caught in the middle of many precarious situations. On one hand, your children or teens are still at home making demands, testing limits, and struggling to go from dependence to independence. On the other hand, your parents, who have been successful and healthy most of their adult life, are now making demands, testing limits, and struggling as they go from independence to dependence. In the middle of this situation is you, the adult child, coping with rambunctious kids, successful careers, and aging parents.

REALITY SETS IN

For many of us, this prime life stage is the most productive as careers soar and children begin to require less attention. Earning capacity is now at its peak and freedom to travel or relax becomes a reality . . . until the phone rings.

"Is this John Peters?" a stranger asks.

"Yes," you reply. You take another sip of your morning coffee as you read the stock market and wonder why anyone would be calling before 7:00 A.M.

"Is this John Peters, the son of Anna J. Peters?" the strange voice continues.

Son of Anna Peters? At that point your heart begins to race, your face becomes flushed, and your voice quivers; you know something is wrong. "Yes, Anna is my mother. Who is this? What has happened to her?"

"This is Franklin County Memorial Hospital calling, Mr. Peters. We are calling to tell you that some time in the past thirty-six-hours your mother fell in her apartment. A neighbor tried to call her all last night and phoned the police at about 5:00 A.M. They unlocked the door and the emergency vehicle brought her to us."

Thoughts of your seventy-four-year-old mother lying in a hospital four hundred miles away without any family member nearby fill your mind. Wasn't it just last week that you detected a weakness in her voice and promised that you would go visit soon? "Is she okay? What happened?" you ask.

"Well, for the time being, she is resting comfortably. But, Mr. Peters, you need to come soon. The doctor feels she may need surgery on her hip, and she is elderly."

You write down the number and address of the hospital and numbly go through the phone book to make calls—book a flight to Franklin; call your boss to cancel the presentation to the new client this morning; call your best friend to get a substitute for the tennis finals this afternoon. Then you wake up your wife and kids, explain the situation, and begin packing for the trip. Your teen's sixteenth birthday party today? "But, Dad, you have to be there," she cries. "I'll only be sixteen once in my life!"

As you drive to the airport you feel as if a piece of your life has been suddenly chipped away as you experience feelings of guilt, confusion, and anger. Yes, the reality of caregiving has set in.

KEYS TO WELL-BEING

Despite all our best efforts, the time will come when most of us will step into the world of caregiving. Some adults are shocked when their parents begin to need assistance. "But this is my brilliant father," cried Lucy, the mother of college age teens and daughter of seventy-six-year-old Henry, a retired physics professor who was recently diagnosed with advanced Alzheimer's disease. "I won't accept that he has become like a child now. My dad was my strength. Now where do I turn?"

Many adults act as if their parents were going to live and be healthy forever, without giving the slightest thought that they may become ill or dependent some day. It is often this shock, as John Peters experienced with his mother, Anna, which causes inner turmoil when a serious illness occurs with an aging parent. These adult children "cannot believe that it happened" to their parents. They tell of their parents suddenly going from vital, active adults to frail, helpless human beings.

WE WILL ALL GROW OLD

Before you even begin caregiving, you must come to terms with your own mortality. The simple reality of life is that all of us are going to grow old. We are all going to die. As our parents reach the senior years, our decisions should focus on how we will respond to this aging process—to the guaranteed life changes—that will take place. Most of our aging parents will be faced with limitations as unexpected illness, the death of a spouse or loved one, or declining mobility occurs. These life changes will cause sorrow and sometimes even depression.

We do not have to allow the guaranteed life changes to dominate our thoughts. In fact, this stage in life can be filled with opportunity as we encourage our parents to explore their potential, enjoy their free time, stay active, and interact with others as they have responsibilities only for themselves. The mature adults who are vital in their senior years are those who do not quit on life—no matter what problems they encounter. That is the attitude we have to instill in aging parents!

A story is told of actor George Burns who was asked what his doctor felt about Burns's incredible vitality and longevity. The active Burns smiled and replied, "He died." A quick sense of humor, a positive attitude, and an energized zest for living—not fear of dying—these are the attributes mature adults must have as they enter into the senior years of life. And with the correct knowledge, including active prevention and planning, you can help your parents establish this attitude.

UNDERSTAND THE LIFE CYCLE

To understand the total life cycle, we must look at aging as an ongoing process that takes place throughout a lifetime. No one wakes up at a certain age and decides that they are now "old." Many amazing people are active, alive, and vibrant in their eighties and nineties. Do you wonder what their secret is? Others—perhaps close friends or even your spouse—seem to be "old" in their forties and fifties, having lost their enthusiasm for living.

Age is like that. People really do not grow old by living a certain number of years. Old age is of the mind. People grow old when they quit taking risks in their lives, when they lose their zest for waking each morning, when they ignore their dreams and allow their lives to become mundane and lackluster.

Unlike the young adult who constantly explores his potential or the middle adult who is in the process of reexamining his life, our parents are at the life stage where they must live with the many choices made throughout their lifetime. For many mature adults, those dreams that began years ago are now a reality as they capture their creativity in hobbies, second careers, church activities, travel, volunteering, and other meaningful uses of free time. Many mature adults realize new dreams as they discover hidden talents and meet new friends. Yet for some of our parents, the adage "nothing ventured, nothing gained" becomes a reality as their retirement years are spent dwelling on nagging ailments or in mundane activities because of lack of personal planning and prevention.

MATURE YEARS ARE FOR DISCOVERY

Often mature adults put aside those dreams that began in their younger years, and form a new dream. Gifted artist Grandma Moses did not even begin her career until age seventy-six and had even painted twenty-five works the year *after* her one hundredth birthday! While she may have been considered "old" by society's standards, she was actually quite young in following her new dream and living each day with expectation.

How our parents handle this life stage will depend a great deal on their attitude and the attitude of those around them. Attitude really governs one's total well-being, allowing for continued growth in the mature years. Depression can also cause many mature adults to feel quite limited by the number of years left in their life calendar. They begin to dwell on these limitations and worries such as declining mobility, a fixed income, or fear of health problems. This depression and worry can contribute to many stress-related diseases. In fact, studies show that more than 80 percent of all illness may be affected by stress in some way. Yet for those aging adults living their senior years to the fullest, these limitations are accepted as part of the changing lifestyle. These adults do not dwell on their limitations, but on their capabilities, talents, wisdom, and especially the knowledge gained through the many years of life.[1]

MY PARENT, MY TURN

As an adult child facing this new life stage as caregiver to aging parents, you need to learn about the many changes your parents will face, including physical and emotional changes, financial changes, changes in residency and independence, and change of position in the family. You must learn how to set limits as a caregiver, so that your tasks do not strain your physical or emotional health or your relationships with family members, friends, and employer. This book will help you do these things.

Through the upcoming years you will witness your parent becoming less independent and more dependent; the person whom you once asked for guidance will become more dependent on you for direction and authority. Your expectations will determine the path your life will take as caregiver to aging parents. Whereas your life may have revolved around spouse, children, and career, you will now experience new demands from another area—aging parents. One study reported that 13 percent of the women interviewed considered "caring for aging parents" as one of their top ten stressors.

But it does not have to be this way! As you become knowledgeable about the realities of aging, you can learn to accept them as

---

1. Harris H. McIlwain, et al. *50+ Wellness Program* (New York: John Wiley and Sons, Inc., 1991), 304.

part of God's natural plan. Then you can begin the planning and prevention of common problems—before they occur.

Our Call to Love

God admonishes us to love one another. Throughout the Bible are passages that teach us how to love through the example of Jesus Christ. Perhaps this is the most profound: "And this commandment we have from Him, that the one who loves God should love his brother also" (1 John 4:21).

We are called to love, and compassion is the style of the Christian—loving out of the love of God, loving with the love of God, continuing to love until we give up the last ounce of our being on behalf of the kingdom. But that wears us out. We get tired, we grow weary, and we see no end in sight. Someone is always standing by to be loved. A loved one is always demanding more.

With all the calls to "go the second mile," a deep and unquestioned urge within us tells us we have to do it—we have to give that cup of water in Jesus' name. The call to love demands our energy. It drains us of power. And so, we grow weary. We suffer compassion fatigue.[2]

But Are You Good Enough?

Good enough is a term we all become familiar with as we raise our children. We try to be the best we can be and may even experience *burnout* as we work toward the goal of "super parent."

"Good enough," as it pertains to caregiving, means that we must now learn to maintain balance. When a parent starts demanding more from you than you can give, feelings of guilt can take over. "My three brothers are no help at all, and they just don't understand," Julia, a forty-three-year-old mother of three, told us. "I have gone over to Mother's home every day for two weeks to make her dinner and straighten up. Since Dad died last year, I feel like the only child who cares anymore. But I need a break; I feel so anxious inside. I want to be a good daughter, wife, and parent to my own children. Where do I draw the line?"

2. Maxie Dunnam, *The Workbook on Coping as Christians* (Nashville: Upper Room, 1988), 135.

Feeling overwhelmed and questioning where "to draw the line" as Julia did are normal. Most caregivers experience this. But before these feelings of guilt and resentment become a reality in your life, you must reevaluate the caregiving situation and make some necessary adjustments, balancing your parent's needs with the needs of your family. No one—we repeat, no one—can be an exceptional parent to their children, a loving and loyal spouse, *and* a super caregiver to their parents without having balance.

If you try to achieve perfection in all areas of your life, everyone—including your parents—will suffer. Perfectionism can be a burden when you do not allow yourself the risky necessity of making mistakes, and as a caregiver, just as a parent, you will probably make mistakes.

As a human being you are imperfect, and yet as a person of faith you are pressing on to become something more than you are now. Knowing this tension, you can begin to make some changes in your expectations of just how much you can give. These changes can help you relax so that you can enjoy God's grace at work in you as you seek wholeness and balance in all areas of life.

BEING BALANCED IS "GOOD ENOUGH"

Carol R., an energetic sixty-one-year-old woman, is a full-time third grade teacher. She also has her diabetic eighty-five-year-old mother living in her home. Carol chose to care for her mother and enjoyed having her in the home—until last summer. Last summer, Carol's husband, Bud, was diagnosed with heart disease. He recently underwent angioplasty for a blocked coronary artery and is now recuperating at home. "I feel like I'm being bounced back and forth with no hope of stopping," she told us. "I go from being a teacher full of energy to a child and wife who feels as if the entire world is sitting on my shoulders. I feel run down, and I know I'm depressed."

Carol is a prime example of a caregiver in crisis. Carol goes the extra mile in everything she does, but she feels that she cannot do enough now to please anyone, especially herself. But with some education and through a caregivers' support group at her church, Carol is learning to step back, reevaluate her situation and seek assistance. In order to cope with the overwhelming responsibilities that have fallen on her, she needs to examine what tasks she can do effectively and what tasks she cannot. This is the point where being "good enough" comes in. "Good enough" mandates that caregivers do their best but also realize personal limitations. A worn out caregiver is of no value to anyone, including himself!

Why Did This Happen to Me?

"Why me?" Lou, a fifty-year-old bookkeeper, asked. "I just packed up my youngest child for college last September and looked forward to traveling, volunteering at my church, and spending quiet evenings with my husband, Sam. Then my seventy-nine-year-old father died suddenly. My mother, who is not well, went into a deep depression, and since last year, I have alternated each evening for months between my mother and Sam. Oh, Sam is angry that I'm never home, and my mother cries when I'm not there that she is so lonely. What about me? Doesn't anyone care about me anymore? I have no life at all."

This feeling is very common, especially when a change in your loved one's condition or needs seems to compound the everyday stresses of working, marriage, and family. Caregiving to aging parents can often push you past what you may feel is humanly possible.

These questions of "why" and feelings of personal loss are very normal and to be expected. The feeling of loss comes from the realization that the nurturing parent you grew up with has changed, and you will *never* have your parent as you knew him or her back again. The parent that cared for you as a child, gave you empowerment and strength, and helped guide you has changed, as has your role in the family. Even though your parent is alive, you feel a significant loss for the one who raised you.

Anger is a normal reaction. Anger is another natural reaction to caregiving, but one that varies from one person to another. Some use the anger in a positive manner, some ignore the anger, and some let these angry feelings consume their whole being. "I resent my parents, my sister, and my husband," fifty-nine-year-old Josalyn told us. "I feel as if I never had time to be me. I married early at age nineteen, and then had four children. I was getting used to my new freedom three years ago when my parents decided they could not live alone. My sister lives six hundred miles away and is not close to the family anymore. Where else could they go? I'm the only one in the family who opened up her home. Now every day I entertain Mom and Dad and make sure they get fed. They are perfectly healthy, but frail. When will I get a turn at life? Some days I feel like my life is already over."

Anger, as Josalyn expresses, can be a normal feeling for caregivers—especially if the responsibility is twenty-four-hours a day without reprieve from siblings or home care. If you identify with anger, this book can help you learn when and how to seek assistance for yourself. This respite will ensure that your life stays balanced. You can replace the energy you spent being angry with positive actions to make your life enjoyable for you and those around you.

Coping with Loneliness. Many primary caregivers also talk about the overwhelming feeling of loneliness. "I never have time for myself," said Maria, mother of three teenagers and caregiver to her eighty-one-year-old mother. "All during the week, I seem to give to everyone—except myself. I want to talk about it with my husband or even children, but I feel that no one understands these feelings of emptiness and loneliness. Who do I turn to for support?"

Caregiving is not easy, and many adults have overwhelming feelings of being all alone. As you continue through this book, you can learn how to make time every day to evaluate your responsibilities, prioritize them, and set attainable goals—goals that do not sacrifice your personal life or your parents' well-being.

PREVENTING COMPASSION FATIGUE

When taking on the new responsibility of caregiving, you must realize that no one is perfect; compassion fatigue or burnout does not have to be ongoing. It is healthy to understand that the best you will ever be is "good enough." You must let go in one area of your life to meet needs somewhere else. At times you may not be able to visit your parent when she needs you because your child has an important event at school. Sometimes you must forego the needs of your parent to be with your spouse and maintain a healthy marriage. Other times you may have to give up responsibility at work, take family leave, or use your vacation days to care for your parent. Cindy, the parent of two teens and caregiver to her eighty-nine-year-old father, said, "Last year was the toughest time in my life. My father had gone into a deep depression after my mother passed away, and he was finally getting well. But on the night of my oldest daughter's senior prom, he called crying and begged me to come to his house because he was lonely. I was so torn yet so tired. I had been with him so many nights, and this was a special time for my family. I had to make a difficult decision that day and let Dad know I could not come. I've never forgotten that moment."

This type of personal conflict is nothing new to those in the position of caring for families and aging parents. Caregiving turmoil can cause relationship problems with your spouse, family upheavals with kids, and difficulties at work, because everyone has certain expectations of you. However, if you anticipate this conflict, you can learn to deal with the problems that you can control, and keep your life balanced as you give "enough" to those you love.

PREVENT PERSONAL DECLINE

As you give time to caregiving, do not ignore your personal needs. You need frequent times alone as you care for so many different people. When a caregiver, whether to children or elderly parents, ignores personal needs, burnout may result. Burnout is a state of physical and emotional exhaustion quite common among persons who are constantly nurturing others. Ministers, nurses, physicians, social workers, and caregivers are usually the victims of burnout. Here are typical symptoms of caregiving burnout:

- negative and rigid attitudes

- dread of starting a new day

- difficulty in sleeping

- irritability and bursts of anger

- lack of energy or enthusiasm

- feelings of being overwhelmed

- no sense of humor

- loss of interest in family, career, or pleasure

- easy to anger

- tired or chronically fatigued

As burnout occurs, you may become apathetic or resentful of juggling too many responsibilities. You may feel tired and drained of enthusiasm.

Kate, mother of two elementary-age boys and full-time nurse, said, "I work the early shift at a local hospital so I can go to my elderly parents' home in the early afternoon to help them get to appointments, change their linens, and fix dinner. By the time I get home at 6:00 P.M. each day, the boys are out of control, and my husband, Paul, is waiting for dinner. Some days I feel that if one more person makes a demand on me I will leave. I can't help it, but I feel emotionally and physically drained every day."

Feeling drained like Kate is a major symptom of burnout. Another sixty-eight-year-old woman who cares for her elderly ninety-year-old mother said, "I feel horrible but lately when my grandchildren come over to visit, I resent the little annoyances that occur with kids—the giggling during supper, asking for another glass of water at bedtime, and the constant questions," Verna said honestly. "I admit that I feel overworked and underappreciated, and sometimes I even resent my grandchildren, although I love them dearly."

Perhaps you have resented the very people you want to love. One lawyer said that after going through a rough weekend with his elderly mother who had Parkinson's disease as well as trying to prepare for a trial on Monday morning, he thought he could no longer make it.

"My world seemed to be caving in, and I felt so all alone," Peter said. "Then I remembered a Scripture our pastor had read last Sunday from Psalm 69. 'Save me, O God! The water is up to my neck; I am sinking in deep mud, and there is no solid ground; I am out in deep water, and the waves are about to drown me. I am worn out from calling for help and my throat is aching' (Ps. 69:1–3)."

After crying for a few minutes, Peter began to realize that he was not the first person in the world who had ever felt overwhelmed with life. He knew that he had to get in control and that God could help him do that.

BURNOUT IS A VICIOUS CYCLE

Caregivers today face many problems coping with kids, careers, and aging parents. First, children still living at home may sense the parent's distraction as they care for problems outside the home and reflect it by becoming apathetic or uncontrollable. Juanita brought her elderly mother to live in their home when she was in the last stages of Alzheimer's disease. "Our youngest child, Sara, was ten years old when Mom came to live with us," she said. "Everything seemed fine at first, but as Mom's sense of reality diminished and she started to ask for her childhood friends to come to imaginary tea parties, Sara became frightened. Sara would not invite any of her school chums to come over the entire year until Mom died, and she distanced herself from Mom and me. I could not put Mom in a nursing home, but I feel so guilty now that Sara lost part of her childhood."

Psychologists advise persons confronted with burnout to listen to the warning signs from the body. Signs of stress such as rapid heartbeat, stomach aches, headaches, or other bodily symptoms can alert you to a problem. Before the symptoms reveal that the body is under pressure, you should evaluate your obligations and pace yourself in this new chapter of family life. To handle the many demands of caregiving, you have to learn to take control of your life instead of letting the demands of life control you.

VERBALIZE YOUR FEELINGS

To achieve balance in your life as caregiver, it is important to get in touch with your feelings. Talk about the pressures of caregiving with your spouse, a close friend, your pastor, or a mental health counselor. Nothing can be clearly resolved without open discussion. Realize that negative feelings are normal. No relationship is immune to resentment or anger.

John, a small business owner, father of three teens, and only son of eighty-one-year-old Minda, feels confident that negative feelings can be expressed in an appropriate manner.

"I have found it necessary to identify the emotions and what triggers the anger inside me," John said. "I work twelve-hour days and then try to stop by my mom's house to see if she has any needs. My next stop is usually the baseball or soccer field to watch the boys play. By the time I get home at night it is around 10:00 P.M. Naturally, my patience runs thin by that time.

"Because of the many demands of my life, I try to talk out my feelings before an explosion occurs—with my wife, the boys, or my mom. Once I identify the initial cause of anger, anxiety, or resentment, I can begin to handle these feelings constructively without hurting anyone.

"Just last month my wife, Peg, and I wanted to go away for the weekend," John continued. "We both needed a break and looked forward to spending three nights at the beach. The boys were great, but when I told Mom I would be away for a while she became upset. I realize now that any time there is change in our routine, Mom becomes agitated and apprehensive as if something horrible is about to happen. But I also know that once we begin to talk about the change and identify what could happen during this time, she begins to relax."

TAKE CARE OF YOUR OWN NEEDS

To remember that one is a person first and a caregiver second is important in living a balanced life. Consider the following scenarios that caregivers face every day. How would you respond?

- You just returned home from a long day at work, and your child reminds you that open house is at her new high school tonight. You fix a quick dinner for the family, write a note to your husband who is still at work, and get ready to fly out the door when the phone rings. Your parent is crying, saying that her ankle has a sharp pain. She mentions that it has been hurting for several weeks, but she did not want to bother anyone. Your daughter is in the car honking the horn, excited about visiting her new school. What do you do?

- Your boss stops by your desk at 5:00 P.M. and asks if you would mind working Saturday morning to help with the inventory. You agree, hoping to get that promotion you have waited for. Then you remember that Saturday is the day that you promised your seventy-five-year old father you would take him fishing. He is recovering from a stroke and has looked forward to this first outing for weeks. What do you do?

- It is your twenty-fifth anniversary, and you sit down for a much-needed leisurely dinner with your husband. Ever since Mom moved to the nursing home, you have stayed with her each night to get her acclimated. Just as you start to relax and enjoy your meal, the supervisor at the nursing home calls to let you know your mother is agitated, refuses to take her medication, and they want you to come immediately. Your husband asks, "Can't it wait? What about us?" How do you handle this?

- You have been feeling very tense ever since Dad had the heart attack, and you made a promise that you would get into a walking program to avoid any stress-related illness. You are making great progress, blocking off a thirty-minute segment of personal time each day when your wife greets you in the driveway. "Your dad is on the phone," she says, "and I think he wants to talk." You go in and try to comfort him. But this happens the next three nights, always at the same time during your time-out. How do you handle this?

Problems Will Happen

Problems like this will confront you frequently as you take on the role of caregiving to an aging parent. What do you do? How do you handle this? If you always choose to put the needs of others—your children, your spouse, your parents—ahead of your personal needs, you will experience compassion fatigue. If you choose to put your own needs ahead of others, you wonder if you will not be acting in a responsible manner.

The most important truth caregivers can learn is that we cheat our parents, our spouses, and our children if we ignore our own needs. Before you read any other chapter in this book, you must understand that a balance must exist between self-care and other-care. We have been given the Great Commandment in the Gospels, "Love your neighbor as you love yourself" (Mark 11:31). This verse presupposes that we love ourselves. If we are full of personal tensions, anxieties and resentment, perhaps we are not loving ourselves enough. Unless we care for self, we may not be adequate to love and care for our families and our aging parents.

Watch Out for Traps

As you begin to take care of aging parents, you will find different "traps" that may occur.

Spouse Trap. Your spouse may become jealous of the time and energy you put into parent care. He or she may give you ultimatums or even refuse to be a part of this new avenue in your life.

Kid Trap. Children who are living at home when caregiving to aging parents begins also may act out their feelings, usually in ways that are not pleasant or acceptable. Your children may become more resentful and rebellious and might even try negative maneuvers to regain your attention.

Parent Trap. Aging parents may also trap you emotionally. Because of the loss of control they may feel they can try to make you feel guilty for not spending enough time with them. They may let you know that they have no money because they spent it all on your college education twenty-five years ago, or they may tell you that these are their "last days" though the doctor told you they were perfectly healthy last month.

Employer Trap. Because you are at the high point of your career, your employer depends on you for knowledge and experience. This person may frown as you take time off to be with your parent, and he may even threaten your job security if you do not place your career as top priority.

If you work toward becoming an informed caregiver, you can act knowledgeably and perceive these traps before they take hold and devastate your life. You can learn how to block out time for yourself so that you are a "good enough" husband or wife, parent, employee, and adult child. (Remember "good enough" is all you can be!) This is the attitude caregivers must take. We realize our limitations, do what we can, and allow others to help.

TAKE TIME FOR YOURSELF

Most caregivers live for that moment when they can close the door at night and shut out the problems of the day. Especially for those meeting the unending demands of children, a busy career, and aging parents, being alone replenishes the strength necessary to cope with problems.

The Bible has a wealth of insight into the need to be alone. Being alone, as indicated by the life of Jesus, need not be a time for feeling sorry for oneself. It can be a time for finding meaning in one's life. When Jesus was in solitude, He found His source of power. After spending the day preaching to and teaching the vast crowds, He "went up a hill by Himself to pray" (Matt. 14:23). Jesus spent time teaching and nurturing the people, and then He "would go away to lonely places where He prayed" (Luke 5:16).

At the beginning of each week, mark down time each day that you can be alone. This could be an hour each evening after your spouse and children are in bed, or it may mean waking up early each morning before they arise. During this quiet time, reflect on the past week and sort through the busyness of your schedule. If you find it difficult to relax during this time, try the relaxation response described in chapter 9 until you begin to feel in control.

Seek Help

Respite care or assistance can help when the pressures of caregiving begin to overwhelm us. A retired couple may enjoy being substitute caregivers for your parents as you and your family take a weekend for renewal. A college-age student may enjoy a chance to become a close friend with your parents in exchange for room and board. Interview these sitters and make sure their values and methods of caregiving are appropriate. Then keep their telephone numbers handy and use them often before the role of "caregiver" becomes overwhelming.

Divide Responsibilities with Siblings and Family Members

To alleviate the mounting caregiving pressure, you will need to organize caregiving with a family meeting. With your siblings and family members, decide how much help your parents need at the moment, and distribute the responsibilities between you. It may be that one sibling lives near the parents and can provide emergency care, while the other siblings contribute to a fund for home care (as discussed in chap. 3). Establish a chart of specific tasks that your aging parents need help with and how they are to be done so the family can continue to run smoothly. Have various family members fill in the blanks to make sure these needs are met. It has been said that youth give hope to the elderly, and the elderly give wisdom to youth. Make sure your children and teens are involved in caregiving so they learn compassionate skills.

A word of caution: You must know upfront that in most families one special person will serve as primary caregiver for an aging parent. If you have that role, you may have siblings or other immediate family members who have been unwilling to make the necessary sacrifices that accompany caregiving. If you are considering the primary caregiver role, be aware that disagreements, denial, and even, at times, severed ties with the family may occur if you try to divide responsibilities with siblings. Whether you ask for help with household chores, transportation to doctors' appointments, or finances, you may find that brothers and sisters who were once close friends want nothing to do with caregiving. As much as you might try to involve everyone in helping an aging parent, it is only natural that the more compassionate will take the leadership. Knowing ahead of time that there could be friction will enable you to continue on with plans for your parent's health, safety, and well-being paramount in your mind.

USE SUPPORT GROUPS

A caregiving support group can be most helpful, especially if you are feeling overwhelmed. This group is composed of adult children who meet together regularly to share caregiving problems, receive support, and enjoy friendships. Meaningful Scriptures can provide biblical guidance for group members.

The caregiving support group should serve as a tool for adult children who need assistance or a sounding board, allowing people to verbalize their problems in an open environment. These problems are not always related to caregiving, but can include the numerous life issues that surmount and complicate the caregiving issue—coping with kids, helping spouses to understand the elderly parent's needs, dealing with work-related demands, and more.

Getting involved in a caregiving support group also has the added benefit of nurturing important relationships. Especially when adults are too busy working all day and caring for children and aging parents at night to cultivate outside friendships, this group provides an important social outlet and offers skills and strength.

Seek professional guidance. The minister of your church is an excellent resource for support and guidance as you become entwined in the web of caring for aging parents while working and raising children. If your problems seem insurmountable, your pastor can recommend professional help and resources, including psychologists, social workers, a local council on aging, a geriatric care manager, and more. You must learn to clear your mind so you can handle daily concerns. A counselor can help you in setting priorities with your career, family obligations, and parent's needs. This support will enable you to set limits and create balance.

Caregiver Bill of Rights

We have given you some pertinent information as to the many demands you will face as caregiver to aging parents. As you begin to understand the new demands on your life, it is important to know your caregiving rights. You have the right to:

1. take care of yourself, as this will help you take better care of your relative.

2. seek help from others, even if your relative only wants help from you.

3. maintain your own interests and life, including paying attention to career and family needs.

4. get angry and express your feelings.

5. reject attempts by relatives to manipulate you through anger, guilt, or depression.

6. receive consideration, forgiveness, affection, and acceptance for what you do for the loved one.

7. offer consideration, forgiveness, affection, and acceptance to others.

8. take pride in what you are accomplishing and applaud the courage it takes to meet the needs of your relative.

9. maintain a full personal life so that when your relative no longer needs you, you will not be lost.

10. continually look for new ways to lighten the load, meet the daily changes that happen, and secure help for your parent and yourself.[3]

Remember, your expectations of the upcoming years can determine your daily experiences as a parent, spouse, worker, and caregiver. As you spend time reading the forthcoming chapters, you will find practical and workable tools to help prevent problems of caring for aging parents.

---

3. "Your Caregiver's Bill of Rights," *The ElderCare Letter* (Opportunity Management, Inc., 1994), 2.

2

UNDERSTANDING PHYSICAL PROBLEMS OF AGING

If someone were to tell you right now that your parent could drastically reduce the odds of the most common serious illnesses, such as cancer, coronary heart disease, osteoporosis, or other major health problems, how would you react? Chances are you would treasure this advice and encourage your parent to follow it faithfully. Consider some of the facts:

- More than 520,000 people die each year from heart attacks.

- About 40,500 women die each year from breast cancer.

- Over 30 million Americans are afflicted with osteoporosis (thinning of the bones) and 80 percent of all women over sixty-five years have this.

- Over 20 million Americans suffer from chronic respiratory disease, including emphysema and chronic bronchitis.

- More than 37 million people suffer from arthritis.

- Unhealthy lifestyle accounts for up to 50 percent of the deaths before age sixty-five.

Research shows that people who take control of their bodies and lifestyle are healthier and make fewer demands for high-cost hospitalization. Some physical changes of aging can be prevented, others must happen whether you like them or not, and several changes cannot be ignored. By understanding the various aspects of aging, you can help your parent prevent problems long before they become an emergency. Your parent can make simple lifestyle changes to stay active and remain healthy in the senior years. When it comes to managing our health, prevention and early detection are the keys to quality of life as we age.

The chances of getting cancer, coronary heart disease, or diabetes could be reduced greatly by eliminating specific risk factors. For example, seniors who get atherosclerosis (hardening and narrowing of the arteries) usually have more risk factors for this disease. Control of those risk factors can make a person much less likely to develop atherosclerosis. Stopping cigarette smoking, reducing stress, and controlling blood pressure and cholesterol may help to prevent heart disease and strokes years later.

Early detection of medical problems allows for treatment when it is easier, most effective, and less expensive. For example, a simple, painless test can detect blood in the stool and allows early treatment of cancer in the intestine long before it causes any other signs. A mammogram (a breast x-ray) may detect breast cancer before any other signs are present, often allowing treatment before the cancer has a chance to spread. A blood test can tell if your parent's blood glucose is high, a signal of diabetes, and could save your parent's life.

While it is not practical to test for all possible medical problems, you can focus on certain medical problems most likely to occur as your parents age. Your parents can maintain their current health or even improve it if they make important lifestyle changes. It will also allow them to manage their future health in a reasonable way, with a minimum time and cost.

Early Detection and Prevention

One example of early prevention is with osteoporosis. This thinning of the bones happens to more than 80 percent of all women by age sixty-five. But did you know that many women have osteoporosis and do not even know it until a fracture occurs?

Elma, a sixty-nine-year-old woman, was brought to our clinic by her forty-eight-year-old son, Pete. She had fallen in the bathtub at their home and had severe hip pain. Elma was found to have a fracture of the hip (femur) and required a hospital stay of ten days with an operation to allow the hip to heal properly. The hospital bill alone was more than $30,000! This is one example of why your parent must understand the most common health concerns of aging and learn how to take steps to eliminate any possible risk factors. Remember, measures taken now can stop the progression and cost of many diseases and problems.

History and Physical Examination

To prevent and detect diseases in early stages so that they can be treated, a complete health history and physical examination is recommended for all senior adults. This should be repeated yearly or as often as a doctor suggests. The visit will include most of the following items:

- A complete medical history, including a discussion of any current and past medical problems.

- A review of recent feelings and symptoms.

- Discussion as needed of drugs, nutrition, areas of stress, alcohol, tobacco, and drug use.

- A complete physical examination.

- Laboratory tests including a complete blood count, blood chemistries including cholesterol and glucose, urine testing, and (depending on your parent's situation) a chest x-ray or electrocardiogram. (Chest x-ray and electrocardiogram are no longer considered a necessary part of a physical examination for adults every year.)

- A review of your parent's current risk factors for coronary heart disease, cancer, and in women, osteoporosis.

- A discussion of recommendations for removal or control of any risk factors possible.

- If any problems are found, then suggestions for further studies and needed treatment, and plans for follow-up of the problem.

- Education about any risk factors and new problems found. Also, a discussion of any other questions or concerns that would help your parent's understanding of his own health situation.

- Hearing examinations, skin test for tuberculosis, and other tests, depending on the individual situation.

- A complete dental and eye examination, if needed.[1]

IMPORTANT RISK FACTORS

The most common causes of serious illness and death for older adults are due to atherosclerosis, which results in heart attack, heart failure, stroke, and kidney failure. The risk factors that can predict a higher chance of heart attack are listed in the chart below. The more risk factors your parent has, the greater the chance of heart attack and atherosclerosis; the fewer risk factors, the lower the risk.

The good news is that the risk can be lowered if each of the risk factors are identified and controlled. For example, studies show that the risk of heart attack and stroke can be reduced by one half or more simply by proper treatment of hypertension alone. While some risk factors for heart attack such as being a male or having a parent who had the disease cannot be changed, your parent has control over certain risk factors.

HEART ATTACK AND HEART FAILURE

Coronary heart disease is the most common type of heart disease. Over 1.5 million people suffer heart attacks each year, and over 500,000 people die each year from heart attack. The risk of heart attack increases with age in men and women.

---

1. Harris H. McIlwain, et al. *The 50+ Wellness Program*, 62.

Heart attack is much more common in men than in women from ages thirty to forty, but by age sixty-five, the rate of heart attack in women catches up to the rate in men!

Rate of Heart Attack

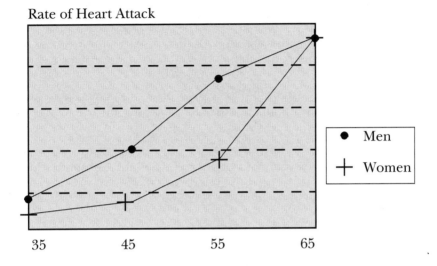

Reduce Risk Factors

Controlling risk factors such as hypertension, high blood cholesterol, and cigarette smoking can greatly lower the risk of heart attack for your parent. The good news is that it is almost never too late in life to take steps to lower these risks. For example, control of hypertension and high blood cholesterol have been shown to lower the risk of heart attack up to around age eighty.

Talk with your parent about the risk factors on page 33. Which ones can they control? Can they try to eliminate these? Remind them that if they can take charge of lifestyle changes, they will greatly reduce the chance of having a heart attack.

One sixty-eight-year-old man, Thomas, became worried when he noticed discomfort in his chest that lasted a few minutes at a time and came on when he walked up the stairs of his condominium. He ignored the feeling for a few weeks, but after the pain started when he was walking to his car, he became worried enough to go to a clinic for a medical opinion.

Thomas had many risk factors for heart attack, including being forty pounds overweight, a blood pressure reading of 185/100 and blood cholesterol of 305, with LDL cholesterol 200 and HDL cholesterol 40. While Thomas had cut back on cigarettes to only a few per day over the last month because of worry about his condition, he had still been a smoker for more than thirty years.

An exercise electrocardiogram (ECG) test showed that Thomas had the same chest discomfort with abnormal changes on ECG which suggested heart problems. He had a coronary arteriogram and was found to have a major blockage of the left anterior descending coronary artery. Balloon angioplasty was scheduled, and since then he has not had any further chest discomfort.

After these treatments, Thomas made some changes. He has lost most of the extra pounds, takes medication to control blood pressure and cholesterol, and hopes to be able to eliminate some of the medication with continued diet and weight loss. He also began an exercise program by walking, which has helped the weight loss. The exciting news is that Thomas tells of feeling better than he has in years.

Thomas's risk of heart attack was about twenty times higher than normal when he started treatment. By stopping cigarettes and controlling hypertension and cholesterol levels, he dramatically reduced his risk in the future. He was fortunate that he sought treatment before a major heart attack caused permanent limitation or even death. Now his future retirement years look positive and hopeful.

Another patient, Pat, was not as lucky as Thomas. This once-healthy, active woman was seventy-four-years old when her daughter found she had collapsed in the garden behind her home. The cause of death was found to be heart attack. As in about half the cases of heart attack, such as Pat experienced, sudden death occurs before reaching the hospital.

PREVENT TRAGEDIES

Is there any way to prevent the tragedy of sudden death? Studies show that a large proportion of cases such as these may have some warning signs such as chest discomfort, which are ignored or overlooked. Although sudden death in an otherwise totally healthy woman or man with no risk factors can happen, it is very uncommon. When examined closely, most of these cases had hypertension, abnormal cholesterol, cigarette smoking, or some combination of these risk factors.

In up to one third of all cases, heart attack is the first sign of heart disease. If your parent does not check his own risk factors, he will miss a great opportunity to prevent heart attack and even sudden death. No one wants to look for trouble, but to ignore the heart risk factors might be compared to putting his head in the sand.

Risk Factors for Heart Attack

- High blood pressure (hypertension)

- High blood cholesterol

- Cigarette smoking

- High fat diet

- Lack of exercise

- Overweight

- Stress

- Personality

- Sex and menopause

- Age

- Diabetes mellitus

- Family history

CONTROL BLOOD PRESSURE

One main risk factor for heart attack is high blood pressure, and the steps for good blood pressure control can be easy.

Have your parent check his or her blood pressure regularly and compare it to the chart on the next page. If the blood pressure remains above the normal level, then steps should be taken to control it. Hypertension can be treated without medication, although in many cases medication may also be needed. A physician will know which measures are the best for your parent's situation.

Some measures, such as eliminating excess salt in the diet, might lower blood pressure even without medication. Other steps to take for treatment of hypertension without medication are listed below.

- Lower salt intake

- Control weight

- Start a regular exercise program

- Manage stress

- Lower excess alcohol intake

- Monitor proper calcium and potassium under direction of a physician (very high intake may be dangerous)

Controlling Hypertension with Medication. If blood pressure does not improve to normal levels after a period of time, then medications may be needed. A doctor can help your parent decide which medication is best suited to control blood pressure with the fewest possible side effects.

Categories of Hypertension			
	Systolic (upper number)		Diastolic (lower number)
Normal Blood Pressure	less than 130		less than 85
High normal	130–139	or	85–89
Hypertension			
Stage 1 (mild)	140–159	or	90–99
Stage 2 (moderate)	160–179	or	100–109
Stage 3 (severe)	180–209	or	110–119
Stage 4 (very severe)	210 or higher	or	120 or higher

The table shows the categories of hypertension of the Joint National Committee on Detection, Evaluation, and Treatment of High Blood Pressure.

Control Blood Cholesterol. High blood cholesterol may be successfully treated with a low cholesterol diet. If diet alone does not control high blood cholesterol, then your parent's doctor can decide whether medication to lower cholesterol should be added. Studies show that it is helpful to control high blood cholesterol up to age eighty to lower the risk of heart attack.

Know Your Parent's Number Total Cholesterol	
desirable	less than 200[*]
borderline high	200–239
high	240 or higher

* This may vary and still be desirable, depending on HDL cholesterol and LDL cholesterol.

LDL Cholesterol	
desirable if person already has coronary heart disease	100 or less
desirable	130 or less
borderline high	130–159
high	160 or higher

HDL cholesterol	
desirable to lower risk	60 or higher
at higher heart risk	less than 35

STOP CIGARETTES

Smoking cigarettes increases the risk of heart attack, but there is a quick drop in risk after stopping. It may be hard to force a parent to stop smoking, even after she fully understands the serious repercussions of this habit such as those listed below. But there are many ways to quit the habit, including individual and group counseling, medications including nicotine patches, and other methods. Talk to your parent's physician for advice.

It would be a good idea to check the risk factors for your parent at least once each year. Then your parent's doctor can give advice on how to control each risk factor. This is a chance to prevent more complicated, limiting, and expensive medical problems and to improve the quality of life for your parent.

Medical Problems Due to Cigarette Smoking

• Coronary heart disease, especially heart attack, heart failure

• Magnifies the risk for coronary heart disease in those who already have high risk from hypertension and high blood cholesterol

• Atherosclerosis and blockage of the arteries that supply the legs—leading to gangrene and amputation

• Atherosclerosis and blockage of the arteries that supply the brain—leading to stroke

• Increased risk of sudden death

• Cancer in the mouth, throat (larynx), esophagus, lung, kidney, bladder, and pancreas

• Blood cholesterol increased by increasing LDL-cholesterol and may decrease HDL-cholesterol

• Emphysema and chronic bronchitis (chronic lung disease)

• Cough, respiratory infections, and asthma illnesses

• May interfere with action of medications given for other medical problems

UNDERSTAND DIABETES MELLITUS

Diabetes mellitus is a medical problem in which the level of glucose in the blood is high. The actual cause is unknown, and no cure is available. However, good medical treatment is available so that the disease is usually able to be controlled and many of its complications avoided.

The abnormal elevation in blood glucose may be found on routine examination, but often persons have feelings of fatigue, weight loss, increase in volume of urine, increased thirst, burning in the feet, changes in vision, infection, or other problems.

After discussion and examination, your parent's physician will plan tests that include blood tests to confirm the diagnosis of diabetes mellitus. Since diabetes mellitus is a risk factor for heart disease, all other risk factors also should be evaluated.

Treatment includes treatment of other underlying problems such as infections. Diabetes mellitus may require insulin treatment to control the blood glucose, and a diet may be prescribed which will allow desirable body weight to be maintained. Close follow up is important to be sure that blood glucose is controlled. Let your parent's physician provide guidance toward treatment to avoid possible complications such as blindness.

CANCER PREVENTION AND EARLY DETECTION

Cancer is a very common source of worry in many older adults, but this worry can be alleviated with knowledge of ways to detect and prevent cancer.

In many cases the most common types of cancer can actually be prevented or detected early when treatment is easier and more effective. For example, lung cancer is the most common type of cancer. But if your parent does not smoke cigarettes, then the chance of this particular cancer is actually very small.

For women, the next most common cancer is breast cancer. Follow the recommended guidelines by the American Cancer Society. This will greatly help to detect early breast cancer, when treatment is less complicated.

Follow the checklist below to find the steps your parent can take to achieve prevention and early detection of the other most common types of cancer. Prevention and early detection measures can be effective and also help give peace of mind to your parent.

Identify and Remove Risk Factors for Cancer

- smoking

- alcohol

- radiation

- chemicals

- hormone treatment

- sunlight (excessive exposure)

- diet (see chap. 8 for healthy diet tips)

Early Cancer Detection Checklist

Senior Women	
Breast examination	Yearly by physician
Self breast examination	Monthly
Pelvic examination	Yearly
Pap test	Every two years up to age 70, then every three years
Mammogram (a type of x-ray of the breast)	Yearly
Senior Men	
Prostate exam	Yearly
PSA test	Yearly
Senior Men and Women	
Rectal examination	Yearly
Stool test for blood	Yearly

Early Cancer Detection Checklist (Continued)

Sigmoidoscopy (direct examination of the rectum, adjacent area of the colon.)	Recommended every five years, but some persons may need this more or less often. Ask your parent's doctor about this particular examination.
Skin changes	Watch the skin for new moles or old ones which change. If any area of the skin becomes darker, new or old moles enlarge or bleed or become painful, your parent should see his or her physician.
Mouth and throat	Report any sores or color changes in the mouth which persist or are painful. This is especially important for persons who use any form of tobacco.
Other	
Eye examination	Yearly for glaucoma, cataract, and other problem
Dental examination	Yearly

OSTEOPOROSIS

Another important area for prevention and early treatment, especially in women, is osteoporosis, which is thinning of the bones (see fig. 2.1).

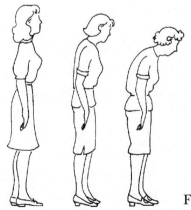

Figure 2.1

Osteoporosis is the main cause of loss of height in the elderly and is the most common cause of hip fracture, one type of the 1.5 million fractures that happen each year from osteoporosis. Hip fractures cost over $10 billion dollars each year. Imagine the savings in suffering and expense if even a small portion of hip fractures could be prevented.

The good news about osteoporosis is that if men and women take steps for prevention, the chances of fractures lessen. One seventy-two-year-old woman we saw got a broken rib when she was hugged by her teenage grandson! She had osteoporosis, and a simple test revealed she had lost about 35 percent of the bone in her lower (lumbar) spine.

She began adding calcium supplements, exercise, and a walking program to her daily routine and was given estrogen and other medications. After two years, repeat tests showed an increase in bone density of 9 percent in her spine. Along with this increase in bone density, her risk of future fractures decreased.

Certain risk factors as outlined in the list below can tell if your parent is at higher risk for osteoporosis, which causes fractures most commonly in the spine, wrist, and shoulder, as well as the hip.

If your parent has more than two risk factors or if there has been a fracture recently, a simple test can determine if osteoporosis is present. The test is painless, simple to perform, and can guide a doctor's treatment of the bone thinning. Treatment is now possible, which may slow the bone loss or improve the bone strength in osteoporosis. This might result in fewer fractures in the future. Your parent's doctor can guide any decision.

Risk Factors for Osteoporosis

- Lack of regular exercise program

- Menopause in women, especially early menopause

- Age forty or older

- Female sex

- White race

- Cigarette smoking

- Family members who have osteoporosis

- Underweight for height

- Heavy alcohol use

- Certain medications: cortisone-like drugs

- Certain medical problems; such as rheumatoid arthritis, emphysema, chronic bronchitis, hyperthyroidism, some types of stomach surgery, diabetes mellitus, other uncommon problems.

- Low calcium in diet

MEMORY LOSS

Alzheimer's disease, which has no cure at this time, is a cause of great concern for most adults. Many senior adults fear Alzheimer's disease, dementia, and memory loss and want to know the difference between simple forgetfulness and serious loss of memory. Caregivers are concerned when they see their parent with memory failure and often ask if this is the beginning of Alzheimer's disease.

Memory failures are common at all ages and if these do not interfere with activities in our daily lives, then they should be of little concern. For example, young people have occasional memory failures, but they certainly are not concerned about serious memory problems. One patient told us, "If you're twenty years old, you can laugh at memory failures; if you're over fifty, you worry about Alzheimer's disease!"

But if memory failures interfere with daily activities, then there should be more concern. Forgetting about appointments, names, places, or directions to very familiar places may all signal a more serious problem. In fact, loss of memory could be an early sign of a decrease in mental activity and function. If it continues, this decrease is called dementia.

THE MOST COMMON CAUSE OF DEMENTIA

While the most common cause of dementia is Alzheimer's disease, some medical problems may make dementia much worse or even cause it. Sometimes these other problems may be treatable, so check with your parent's doctor to know if this is possible in their case. For example, a serious infection in an older patient may cause confusion, poor memory, and inappropriate behavior, which returns to normal after the infection is treated!

Alzheimer's disease is usually diagnosed after age sixty-five. You can find comfort in knowing that there is no definite evidence that you will develop the disease if your parent has Alzheimer's disease.

THE SIGNS OF ALZHEIMER'S DISEASE

Memory failure is usually one of the first signs of Alzheimer's disease, but this may be barely noticeable for months or years. Other people may notice gradual changes in behavior, thoughtfulness, and warmth of personality, and the person's emotions may lessen. As the disease progresses, the person's judgment, reasoning power, and use of language may become more difficult. Daily business and personal decisions may be made with poor judgment. At this point more direct help is needed in daily decision making. In later stages of Alzheimer's, the person's personality changes.

Activities such as driving a car or even dressing and eating become more difficult, and there may be loss of the control of bowels or bladder. The patient usually becomes severely limited and eventually bedridden. The entire course of the disease may take months, but more commonly it takes several years.

Talk to your parent's doctor about any specific medical problems that may be treatable to help make the condition less severe and less limiting. As much as possible, provide an environment that prevents problems that might aggravate the mental deterioration, such as good nutrition, cleanliness, exercise, and a supportive, caring home.

OTHER PROBLEMS OF AGING

CHRONIC PAIN

Over 100 million people suffer chronic pain. Your parent might have pain from arthritis (pain and stiffness in the joints), back pain, headache, or other causes. Pain adds to the burden of other medical problems associated with aging and often causes less activity. Pain and decreased activity can contribute to depression, which is a common problem even in older persons without pain.

Constant pain can cause a cycle of less activity (because activity hurts), which can bring on depression and even more pain. This can result in fatigue, loss of interest, and difficulty concentrating, all of which may make your parent appear to have a more severe loss of reasoning power. Relief of pain may actually increase activity and alertness.

Pain relief is available for many causes of chronic pain, but first be sure of the proper diagnosis of the causes of your parent's pain. For example, there are over 100 different types of arthritis—the more specific the diagnosis, the better the treatment plan to control the pain and stiffness. Many older patients who suffer from back pain commonly find more than one cause of the pain. The back pain may be due to arthritis or osteoporosis (thinning of the bones), each of which has different and specific treatments. By deciding which problems are contributing to the pain, the treatment can then be much more effective.

ARTHRITIS

Over 37 million Americans are affected by arthritis, and more than half of those over the age of sixty-five have arthritis. The most common type of arthritis is osteoarthritis, often called the wear-and-tear arthritis, which is most common after age fifty. In this problem, the cartilage, which normally cushions the joints, becomes worn and less efficient. There is often pain, swelling, and stiffness in and around the joints.

Osteoarthritis often affects joints that hold the weight of the body, like the knees, hips, and back. The pain is usually worse with activities like walking or standing and improved when sitting and less active. Unfortunately, the joints that allow us to do many of our daily activities are often those most affected.

Rheumatoid arthritis can cause pain, swelling, and stiffness in many joints. It can be a severe and even destructive and crippling arthritis. Treatment is available to delay or stop bone destruction. Other problems can also arise in severe arthritis.

Some Common Joint Problems in Arthritis

- Joint pain

- Joint swelling

- Joint stiffness

- Joint warmth

- Joint redness

Some problems other than joint pain in arthritis

- Stiffness in the morning on arising

- Fatigue

- Weight loss

- Rash

- Discoloration of the fingers on cold exposure

- Sensitivity to the sun

- Loss of hair

- Mouth ulcers

- Neck pain

- Eye dryness and loss of vision

- Chest pain

- Heart disease

- Lung disease

- Kidney disease

- Shortness of breath

- Difficulty swallowing

- Headache

- Hypertension

- Seizures

- Genital ulcers

- Painful urination

- Diarrhea

- Vision changes

- Eye inflammation

- Sinusitis

- Liver disease

- Abdominal pain[2]

Fibromyalgia and soft tissue pain can be a cause of severe pain in the back, shoulders, neck, and other areas. The pain is often felt all over the body. Sleep is usually poor, and fatigue is almost always a problem. There are trigger areas—tender points in the neck, back, and other areas that are very painful to touch. The pain and fatigue of fibromyalgia can be diagnosed by a doctor. Treatment is available, and the earlier it is begun, the better for your parent.

Early diagnosis is best. Early diagnosis is important since good treatment is available for most types of arthritis. A basic treatment program includes moist heat, exercises, and specific medications. In fact, in most cases patients find a medication that gives some relief in arthritis and back pain. With pain relief can come more activity, which in turn can help a person's attitude and alertness. While no cures are available in most cases of arthritis, enough improvement in pain can reasonably be expected to allow desired daily activities.

Mabel, a seventy-three-year-old woman, came to see us because she was feeling pain and stiffness in her knees while playing golf. At first the pain was only occasional after playing eighteen holes, but then it became constant and worsened. She had no other joint pain or stiffness and actually felt well except for the knee pain. This woman was found to have osteoarthritis in both knees. But after starting a regular program of exercise and medication, over a period of time, Mabel told of great improvement in her knee pain and stiffness. She is now back on the golf course without much discomfort.

Another seventy-year-old man, Steven, saw a doctor because of pain and swelling in his fingers. While he had a difficult time moving his fingers, no other joints were affected. Steven felt well, except for the aching pain that kept him from his hobby of woodworking and fixing clocks. After an examination and x-rays, he was also diagnosed with osteoarthritis and began regular treatments at home using a heated paraffin bath. He was given some exercises to strengthen his hands and make them more limber. Steven took an anti-inflammatory medication to help his swollen joints, and after several weeks he was able to continue his hobbies.

While arthritis is common with senior adults, your parent's condition can be managed for a mobile and active lifestyle.

BACK PAIN

Most adults in America have had back pain in the past year. For young and middle-age adults, this most common loss of work except for the common cold is estimated to cost $50 to $75 billion each year.

For senior adults, back pain is a common problem, but the first step in controlling back pain is proper diagnosis to find the true causes of the pain. Your parent's doctor can guide you to the right answers.

Warning Signs. If your parent has back pain for the first time and this pain is severe, a doctor can give advice. If the pain does not lessen after a few days, or if the following warning signs are present, make arrangements to get further medical attention.

- The back pain is worse when he coughs or sneezes.

- The back pain or numbness travels down one or both legs.

- The back pain awakens her from sleep.

- He has back pain and finds it difficult to pass urine or to have a bowel movement.

- The back pain is accompanied by loss of control of urination or bowel movements.

A Basic Treatment Plan. After proper diagnosis, a basic treatment plan can begin. This usually includes the daily use of moist heat such as a warm shower, or bath, or warm towels along with a regular exercise program. Exercises and activity, as discussed in chapter 7, actually help most types of back pain; without them, the back pain usually continues.

Medications are also available that help control back pain. In some cases, medications available over the counter such as Advil® (ibuprofen) or acetaminophen may control the pain. Or your parent may need to use a prescription medication given by the doctor.

Helpful Forms of Moist Heat for Pain

- Heated swimming pool

- Warm whirlpool or hot tub

- Warm shower

- Warm bathtub

- Hot packs as a hydrocollator pack

- Warm, moist towel or cloth

- Moist heating pad

Exercises for Arthritis and Back Pain. Exercise is critical in controlling the pain of arthritis, most types of back pain, and many other types of chronic pain. Exercises, which can easily be done by your parent at home, will help make the joints and back more flexible and limber. They will also help increase the strength of the muscles that support the joints and back, which will help reduce the pain.

In our clinic, we find that those senior adults who stay active and keep a regular exercise program are almost always able to see and feel improvement with their pain. As you will read in chapter 7, there are no specific limits for exercise by age, and most seniors who thought they could never exercise can successfully manage an exercise program. Talk with your parent's doctor about the range of motion exercises. A physical therapist can help with instruction in exercises and can also show the proper positioning for moist heat towels.

Remember, your parent does not have to simply live with back pain or any pain, for that matter. Help them seek answers and find the cause, then begin proper treatment to stop the cycle of pain.

HEADACHES

Headaches, which can be severe and limiting, can also be controlled in senior adults. Some surveys have reported that 70 to 90 percent of all women and men have headaches. Of this number, 40 to 50 percent of women and men report headaches that they regard as disabling. Most common headaches are brief and mild, but others are frequent and severe.

Headaches can stem from many causes, such as arthritis in the neck, tension, vascular problems, temporomandibular joint pain (TMJ), sinus infections, inflammation of the nerves or arteries, and more.

If your parent suffers with headaches, seek medical advice.

Fortunately, most headaches are not of a life-threatening nature, although the pain itself can be limiting.

Once you are sure of the cause of the headache, ask your parent's physician about starting a basic treatment program for the specific cause of the headache.

Depending on the doctor's evaluation, this treatment could include medications, moist heat applied to the neck such as a shower or warm towels, and exercises. Most people find that the combination of medication, exercise, and moist heat enables them to reduce the pain and live an active life.

Urinary Incontinence

Urinary incontinence is the loss of urine control severe enough to be a problem. This happens in 15 to 30 percent of persons over age sixty, and affects 50 percent or more of those in nursing homes. Urinary incontinence is twice as common in women as men. The sad truth is that half or less of those who suffer from urinary incontinence consult their health care provider about the problem. If your parent suffers with this, she may try absorbent pads for protection or simply become limited in activity or homebound. It is important for you to let your parent know that urinary incontinence is not shameful; it is most common in aging adults and can be treated and managed.

Urinary incontinence can put a great burden on the aging adult and his family. Estimated costs exceed $10 billion each year. Incontinence of urine and bowels are often the final events that trigger placement in a nursing home as it makes it more difficult for a person to continue to live with family.

Treatment. Your parent's doctor can help diagnose the type of urinary incontinence and also discover any other underlying medical problems needing treatment. Every person is different, so it is important to get the best treatment available for your parent.

Treatment includes bladder training, in which the person is taught to urinate according to a schedule, usually trying to increase up to two to three hours apart. Some studies have found that 75 percent of women improved with this training and 12 percent reported that they no longer had incontinence.

Other types of behavior training and exercises to increase the strength of the pelvic muscles may also be used, depending on the individual situation. Biofeedback, electrical stimulation of the pelvic muscles or nerves, or combinations of the above may be successful.

Medications. Medications to help incontinence are also available. These can be used after proper diagnosis and along with the other steps discussed above.

If other measures do not work and the urinary incontinence is still severely limiting, surgery may be a consideration. Your parent's gynecologist or urologist is the best guide as to the value of surgery in the individual situation.

Absorbent pads, pants, shields, diapers, and other products can give temporary protection. Just be sure that your parent does not use pads for protection instead of proper evaluation. Since treatment is available, the early use of protective pads might delay discovery of a more serious medical problem, or it might delay treatment that could allow the pads to be used much less or not at all. Some researchers recommend permanent use of pads only after good medical evaluation and failure of other treatments.

TAKE PERSONAL RESPONSIBILITY FOR HEALTH

Once your parent understands the risk factors for major problems that can occur with aging, he or she can take specific steps to eliminate those that can be controlled.

Lifestyle changes combined with early detection and treatment of disease can enable you and your parent to approach the senior years with confidence and assurance.

3

PLANNING FOR CAREGIVING

When Martha P. turned forty last year, she called it the "most horrible, devastating year of her life." According to this busy mother of two and elementary school teacher, not only did she reach a turning point in her own life, but her father did as well. "Here I was trying to cope with my own mortality as I hit the big 4-0, when my seventy-year-old father began to have all sorts of health problems," she said. "These problems were not life-threatening, but he was affected emotionally as were we all that year."

Martha went on to ask: "So how do I know when to seek outside help for my parents? They are only in their early seventies, but they are starting to act fragile. I worry that something terrible will happen when I least expect it."

KNOW WHEN TO INTERVENE

Knowing when to intervene and help aging parents is a dilemma for many families in the nineties. When should you be concerned about your aging parent's health, finances, or living arrangements? When do you seek home care? When do you move a parent to a nursing home or to live in your home? Unfortunately, there are no definite answers to these concerns.

Finding that delicate balance of when to help and when to back off is difficult for adult children as each case is unique. The situation is similar to raising children; there is no owner's manual that applies to every child. You are stepping into a new arena of caring that has no rules or lists of criteria to checkmark.

How do you learn to care for your first baby? Most people read books on the subject, talk to trusted friends, make numerous calls and visits to the pediatrician, and, finally, rely on instinct as they make decisions regarding this new life.

The same holds true when your parents age. You must read on the subject, network with trusted friends, talk to professionals, and then follow your intuition as you find the best way to handle each situation. Adult children often comment, "Every day is a challenge as I never know what to expect." To a degree this may be true; caregiving is a challenge. But just as you gleaned information from many sources to raise children responsibly, you must also become so knowledgeable about the aging process and available services for caregiving that you will know what to expect, how to prevent crises from happening, and how to make decisions that everyone—aging parents and adult children—will benefit from.

COMMON CONCERNS OF CAREGIVERS

The concerns of caregivers are many. These extend from a parent's new loss of independence to worries over health and safety to the increased responsibilities of adult children at a time when they are actively involved in parenting and careers. Rather than wait until a crisis occurs, it is best to get these concerns out in the open, deal with them, then make plans to prevent mishaps from occurring.

FINANCIAL STATUS

One of the main concerns of adult children is the financial status of the parent. Questions frequently asked are:

- How can I offer her money without offending her?

- How do I know if he has enough to make ends meet?

- What if he cannot pay his rent or house payment?

- What if she scrimps on food or fails to purchase medication so she can cover other monthly expenses?

- What if she falls prey to phone scams and gives out her credit card or checking account number?

- What if he fails to use the heater or air conditioner to save money on electricity?

- What if she asks me for financial assistance? Do I tell my children they cannot go to college so that I may help my parents?

Some caregivers notice "signs" aging parents give to let you know that money is tight or, more commonly, that they fear running out of money. One man visited his eighty-one-year-old mother and noticed that she had little fresh food in her refrigerator. "I thought Mom had plenty of money in the bank," he said. "But when I confronted her, she said she was afraid to use it in case she ran out when she got 'old'." Another man told of his father collecting bottles on the side of the highway on weekends. "My father is seventy-two years old, owns his own home, and has a secure retirement. But he told me he was worried that he might need extra money in case he became ill in later years."

LONG-TERM CARE

Long-term care is another concern of most adult children. Questions are asked, such as:

- How will I know when Mom should go to a nursing home?

- Will Dad be able to live alone now that Mom has died?

- Should we ask them to move in with us so they get a hot meal each day?

- Should I take my parents to the adult day care at their church so I can go back to work?

- How can we trust the home care workers to attend to her daily needs?

- What if someone breaks into his home? How can I feel confident that he is safe?

These issues are real. If your parent is comfortable discussing these areas, sit with other family members, and make some tentative long-term plans. Ask about financial resources. Ask about long-term care. If your parents are unable to care for themselves fully, do they want to stay in their own home with assistance, move in with you, or go to a retirement complex? Most adults have definite ideas about their money and their preferred housing. But discussing the topic openly before there is a crisis will allow everyone to plan and prevent some of the problems of aging.

Many families—adult children and aging parents—openly discuss what type of burial they want upon death; some even talk about what they want written in their obituary or what songs or Scriptures they want at the funeral service. Should you discuss this with your parent? That is for you to decide, depending on the openness of your relationship. Your parent will let you know when you have crossed the line as you look into personal needs and desires. Be sensitive to this barrier yet still confident that you understand your parent's situation.

COMMON CONCERNS OF AGING PARENTS

While your immediate concerns may be about finances and long-term care, your parent will probably have different worries. Many elderly adults worry about maintaining their independence, such as the handling of day-to-day tasks, getting where they need to go, and remaining in their home as long as possible.

Loss of transportation is a major fear of the aged, and is a direct blow to remaining independent—the biggest desire of most frail elderly. How will they get to their doctor's appointment (one of the most common places the frail elderly go), grocery store, errands, or church? Losing their drivers' license or car insurance is on their mind daily. And these losses are not a matter of "if" it will happen, but rather a matter of "when."

Other common fears of the elderly including the following:

- fear of illness and death

- fear of loss of independence

- fear of personal losses

- fear of falling

- fear of loss of respect

- fear of being abandoned

- fear of becoming forgetful

- fear of leaving their home

- fear of being a burden

- fear of personal security or safety

Then there are the worries that seem so remote to most people. Little things we all take for granted become of great concern to aging parents, such as changing a light bulb, trimming toenails, cleaning the bathtub, weeding the garden, cutting the hedge, dusting the ceiling fan, moving the furniture, walking outside to get the paper, and more.

It is important to realize that if you do not address your parent's concerns early, you may find him or her leaning on you more and more. By openly solving problems before a crisis hits, you can help your parent meet these needs to stay self-sufficient. Whether the help comes from grandkids on Saturday mornings to a daily homemaker's assistant to adult children taking turns each week to do chores, the more independent your parent remains, the higher the quality of life for everyone.

A Plan for Caregiving

Communication is the key to successful caregiving. To organize for caregiving, discuss with your parents any concerns you may have regarding their lifestyle. If you have noticed any of the common signs of problems listed later in this chapter, be very firm about seeing a doctor for a medical evaluation. If that evaluation is positive, use the suggestions listed to help your parent get in control of his or her life.

As you begin to understand the various caregiving options, your goal as the adult child is to work toward compromise. This does not mean perfection; it means being "good enough." If your parent is safe, healthy, and basically happy, you can feel assured that all is okay. While you may not prevent everything, you can limit and prevent the most common mishaps. Keeping independence is the primary goal as you make this caregiving plan; you can fill in the gaps with support services listed in chapter 4 as problems arise.

SELECTING PROFESSIONALS

Many professionals will play an important role in caregiving to the elderly. This list is lengthy and can include the physician, pastor, attorney, and others such as a home health nurse, social worker, or geriatric case manager. Be sure these professionals are carefully screened. When planning for caregiving, keep all these professionals accessible, in case you need them.

Many issues must be considered when selecting professionals to assist you with caregiving. Make copies of the form in Appendix A. When you interview the professional, use this list, and attach it to the resume as you consider who would best serve your needs.

CHOOSE A FAMILY LIAISON

Choose one family member to be the liaison to these support providers, rather than having various members calling the provider with a different story and question regarding the elderly parent. The family member who is the liaison will make necessary phone calls to the professional relaying pertinent information about the parent. This member should intervene if the parent is not getting adequate care from the provider or if the parent is not an accurate communicator.

Have the family liaison make necessary appointments with the professionals. Be sure to have the list of questions to ask this person. As they give advice—whether medical, financial, emotional, or spiritual—write this advice down in a notebook so you and your parent can go over this later. For many reasons, such as hearing loss, your parent may not understand the instructions given. Having this written information is especially helpful for moments when your parent says, "I don't need to take that medication any more." You can take the notes from the doctor's visit and reply, "Well, you must. Your doctor said it is important for your health. Should we make an appointment and discuss this again?" Having the support of knowledgeable professionals enables you to avoid being the villain and offers protection for those moments when the parent begins to challenge your guidance.

Observations and Concerns

What changes have you noticed in your parent's health, behavior, or lifestyle? Read about the most common changes later in this chapter. Before you talk with the professional, write your observations down along with specific concerns. Mention these to your parent first, instead of surprising them at the consultation with the professional. There may be a reasonable response as to why they have lost weight, have not paid their bills, or avoided family members. If they do not have a logical answer, bring up the observations when you seek assistance.

The following are sample observations and concerns you could mention to a physician, attorney, nutritionist, pastor, social worker, or other. When writing down your observations and concerns, make it simple and direct, use examples, and seek a response.

- Observation: I noticed Dad's refrigerator stocked with the same food I bought him two weeks ago, and none had been eaten.

Concerns: He has lost weight recently. I am afraid he is not eating. Could he be ill? Is he depressed? Should I hire a homemaker's assistant to cook for him? What home care programs are available for Dad at his income and need level?

- Observation: When I call Mom she does not seem interested in talking with me, yet when I visit, she is quite talkative.

Concerns: Could she have a hearing problem? Would a hearing aid help her? Could we have the phone company put a device on her phone to increase the volume of incoming calls? Could hearing loss be the reason she has dropped out of her Sunday School class? Is there a special place she could sit in church so she can hear the sermons?

- Observation: When I got to Dad's home last week, his mailbox was stuffed as if he had not emptied it for days. There were past due bills and even a card from the water company saying they were putting him on notice.

Concerns: Dad seems very slow to react recently. After having him checked out medically, I am still left with a lot of questions. Could he have had a stroke? What shall we do about his finances? Do we need power of attorney to handle his financial affairs? Does the post office have an intervention program that would send me notification should he forget to pick up his mail? Would it help to have someone check on him each day?

GETTING ORGANIZED

After writing down your observations and concerns, let the following professionals assist you in organizing for caregiving.

Accountant. An accountant is important if your parent is no longer able to maintain control of financial assets. The accountant can do the yearly IRS return, evaluate any securities or holdings to see if they are properly invested or disbursed, and consult with your parent about risky decisions. Again, your parent needs to fully participate as much as he is able, and the family liaison should be at the meeting to understand the financial status of the parent.

Attorney. An attorney must understand your parent's legal matters. Choose one who is familiar with legal issues that affect senior adults. The attorney can help your parent in drawing up a will and can provide answers to any questions regarding trusts, living wills, guardianship, and more. Be sure your parent and appointed family liaison meet with the attorney periodically to ensure smooth transition should your parent become ill or die suddenly.

Counselor. Your parent may have emotional or psychological problems and be referred by their primary care physician to seek therapy. The knowledge, support, and professional guidance of a licensed mental health counselor will become important to your parent, spouse, and family members. Whether or not your parent's problems mandate counseling with a psychologist or psychiatrist, this person will become a vital resource for dealing with illnesses such as depression and learning to cope with sadness, loss, and grief.

Geriatric Care Manager. You can hire a geriatric care manager to evaluate your parent's situation and make recommendations. Charges range from $30 to $150 per hour for the evaluation plus the charge of the services, if you choose to use them. The benefit of hiring a care manager is exceptional as this trained person can give you a good evaluation of your parent's strengths and weaknesses and recommend what services would best meet each need. The care manager can tell you and your parent the services your parent would qualify for in your community and the ones you would have to pay for, including current prices (see home care services in chap. 4). Especially if you are long-distance caregiving or if you do not have time to research, interview, fill out papers, and monitor caregivers for your parent, this service offers peace of mind. Care managers are professionals at communication with the elderly. Your parent should be present for the discussions regarding his home care so he will cooperate when the assistance comes. You may find private geriatric care managers listed in the yellow pages under the heading "social services" or "senior," or you can contact your area agency on aging.

Guardian. A guardian is a person who has been appointed by the court to act on behalf of a person. Guardians can be named to make decisions for people about their personal well-being or to manage their assets and income, or both. The guardian can be anyone from a spouse, child or other relative to a state bank, trust company, national bank, or other. Check into the rules in your state to see how this applies in your parent's case.

Home Health Nurse. A home health nurse is a registered or licensed practical nurse who will come to your home, if requested by a physician, social worker, or hospital discharge team, to do evaluations and make recommendations. The nurse can also help elderly persons who are suffering from a chronic disease by assessing their vital signs, taking blood pressure, monitoring blood sugar levels, giving injections, helping with catheters or wound dressings, and more.

Find out if these home health services are covered by Medicare, Medicaid, or your parent's supplemental insurance. Medicare covers some home health services and personal care as long as it meets the guidelines for the diagnosis. Every situation and diagnosis is different, so let the medical professional guide you.

Nutritionist. The physician or home health nurse may request a consultation by a nutritionist regarding the proper diet for your parent's special needs. Make sure the nutritionist is a licensed dietitian, and ask for credentials. The proper diet for varying health problems can make a big difference in your parent's strength and recovery. Problems such as cancer, diabetes, high blood pressure, heart attack, kidney problems, gum and teeth problems, and more can be affected by proper nutrition. Without healthful nutrition, your parent's health can decline rapidly (read chap. 8 for ideas for healthful meals).

Occupational Therapist. An occupational therapist can help your parent learn the best way to do daily living tasks that may have become difficult for various reasons. Assistance with bathing, eating, toileting, walking, and other tasks that require special devices can make the tasks easier and help your parent maintain independence. The occupational therapist can give advice on accessibility in the home and ways to improve the physical plan. People who have arthritis, cancer, stroke, heart attack, emotional problems, mental health concerns, fractures, Parkinsons, amputations, and more could all benefit from an occupational therapist.

Your parent's doctor can direct you to a therapist who can help increase physical strength and endurance, identify community resources, adapt the home for safety and efficiency, help recognize and control depression, as well as other intervention. Payments for these services are available through both Medicare and Medicaid in addition to private insurance.

Pastor. For most Christians, the pastor is an important person in their life, offering spiritual support, hope and strength during illness, death of a spouse or friend, or periods of loneliness. Your pastor should be available twenty-four hours a day. Make certain the family liaison has met with your parent's pastor and discussed the needs so when a phone call is made, the pastor responds accordingly and understands the parent's health and emotional status.

Pharmacist. The pharmacist is another key professional in your parent's life as he or she fills prescriptions, answers questions regarding side effects or how to take medications, and recommends over the counter treatment, if necessary. It is most helpful to have a pharmacist who knows your parent and his or her physician, and to also have access to a pharmacist who works the night shift—in case of emergency. Your parent's pharmacist should fill *all* prescriptions and know *all* medications she is taking to determine if harmful interactions could occur.

Physical Therapist. Lack of exercise, overall weakness, a fractured hip, knee replacement, stroke, and extended bed rest are just a few of the problems the elderly face that could cause them to be unable to walk or to be unsteady in using their arms or legs. A physical therapist can vastly accelerate a patient's recovery. This provider should be recommended by the physician. A referral from your home health nurse or physician is needed to have this service covered by Medicare.

Primary Physician. The primary physician is your parent's main medical provider. This person knows the parent's physical and emotional needs and should do a yearly medical evaluation, referring your parent to specialists as needed. The primary physician should be aware of all medications your parent takes. Again, the liaison should meet or talk with this physician periodically to discuss any new health concerns and how family members should address them. Be sure the liaison takes a bag with all prescriptions when they go to the appointment. Talk with your parent's physician about accepting assignment from Medicare (see chap. 10), and decide upfront how to handle bills and payments.

Social Worker. The social worker is trained to help the family cope with changes due to illness or age. The social worker can evaluate the situation and make recommendations for coping or solving problems, including how to manage personal finances or where to receive housing, benefits, and entitlements. The social worker can help you get through the bureaucratic channels. An added benefit of meeting with this professional is that she is trained to help people cope with a parent's illness or impending death.

Speech Pathologist. Any illness or injury that causes speech, hearing, or swallowing problems could benefit from the assistance of a speech pathologist. Examples would include stroke, brain tumor, head injuries, or other neurological diseases of the elderly. The speech-language pathologist evaluates all areas of a person's speech and language behavior. Information is then provided to the family about the person's ability to speak, write, and read, as well as his or her ability to understand the speech, writing, and gestures of others. All communication areas may not be affected; some areas may be impaired more than others. Your parent's physician can recommend these services.

WHEN TO INTERVENE

As you get organized to help your parent, you must first assess his or her physical, mental, and emotional state. Just as your child gives you clues when something is amiss in his life, so will your aging parents. And these clues will probably be the first signs that intervention is necessary and caregiving must begin.

COMMON SIGNS OF PROBLEMS

The following represent eight common areas of decline for aging adults. If you notice these changes in your parent, be certain to make observations, write down your concerns, and call the necessary professionals for evaluation and guidance.

Declining Hygiene. You may notice your parent is not taking baths, using deodorant, shampooing her hair, or even combing her hair. When you visit you may see that her clothes are soiled or wrinkled or that he no longer shaves his face.

Loss of Weight. You may notice that your parent's clothes seem baggy and the face is drawn. His skin may appear "loose," and her eyes may look sunken or tired.

Confused Demeanor. Your parent may suddenly become forgetful, have slurred speech, or be unable to finish a sentence as he loses his train of thought. She may look at you with a blank stare in her eyes instead of the sparkle she once had.

Poor Housekeeping. You may open the refrigerator and see spoiled food or inadequate nutritious food available. She may not have washed dishes in days, vacuumed rugs, or the sheets may be soiled. His bathroom may be grimy or have strong odors.

Ignoring Medications. When you visit you may see that medications are not being taken or are not being taken properly. You may find that she is unable to open the medications or that he can no longer swallow the large pills and may be confused or forgetful.

Withdrawal. You may see that a parent has changed his pattern of interaction with friends, neighbors, and relatives. He may stop church activities or volunteer work suddenly. You may find that the parent does not wish to talk with you or the grandchildren and prefers to be alone.

Neglecting Mail and Newspapers. You may look outside and find that the mail has not been touched in days or that the newspapers are still on the lawn.

Poor Finances. You may receive notice that your parent has overdrawn her checking account, or collection agencies may send bills regarding payments that are delinquent.

The first step in getting to the root of problems of an aging parent is to check with his physician and request a physical. If your parent is not interested, be firm so the doctor can rule out any medical problems that could be instigating the new behavior. Be sure to tell the doctor about the new behaviors and give any previous medical or emotional history that might be helpful.

After a medical evaluation, you will need to take action so your parent can stay independent while improving these behaviors.

PREVENT POOR HYGIENE

Have a professional rule out any medical problems that may cause poor hygiene. You may notice neglect or a change in cleanliness, dressing, or bathing with parents. Depression may make them withdrawn and careless about their appearance. Or a stroke could cause weakness or trouble with coordination and make it too difficult to bathe or take care of personal hygiene. Dementia can cause aging adults to forget or not care about themselves. These and other medical problems should be detected, since each could be treated and result in overall improvement.

- Let your parent know about your concern, and make an appointment with the doctor to rule out a health problem.

- If he is doing well otherwise, this may mean that you should check on your parent more often.

- If this is the only problem your parent is having at this time, a chart in the bathroom may be a gentle reminder of the daily hygiene needed. Write down the days of the week along the side, and across the top of the chart, write the hygiene areas that need attention. Have him look at this chart daily and checkmark the areas he completes, such as bathing, shaving, shampooing hair, brushing teeth, changing clothes, and changing underwear. Talk about the chart each week and praise your parent for following through.

Sample Hygiene Chart

	Bath	Shave	Shampoo	Teeth	Clothes	Underwear
Monday						
Tuesday						
Wednesday						
Thursday						

Sample Hygiene Chart (Continued)

Friday						
Saturday						
Sunday						

PREVENT WEIGHT LOSS

Again, any medical problem behind weight loss must first be ruled out. In depression the adult becomes withdrawn and loses appetite. Dental problems can make it too hard to chew the food. There could also be a problem swallowing from a stroke. In some cases of dementia or other medical problems, the skills of preparing food may become limited. Or the pain of severe arthritis may make it difficult to stand long enough to prepare food. Medical evaluation can discover any underlying contributions to weight loss and allow appropriate treatment.

- Discuss with your parent the information given in chapter 8 to ensure he is eating the proper nutrients each day. If your parent has a specific health problem, check with his doctor to receive the correct diet or list of nutritional needs.

- Hire a home assistant to help with shopping and meals.

- Have a local restaurant or cafeteria prepare meals once a week and freeze these to be microwaved later.

- Freeze part of your dinner each night and take it to your parent's home weekly.

- Apply for Meals-on-Wheels or another nutritious meals program.

- Make a chart for the kitchen with the days of the week listed. Check with your parent's physician to see how many glasses of liquid are needed each day to prevent dehydration. Discuss some healthful menus with your parent and list these on the chart. Have your parent checkmark this each day as she eats her meals.

Sample Healthful Meal Chart

Monday	cereal, milk, fruit
	tuna salad, lettuce, peaches
	meatloaf, potatoes, green beans, milk
Tuesday	egg on toast, banana
	turkey sandwich, tomato, applesauce
	spaghetti, peas, bread, yogurt
Wednesday	applesauce, toaster waffle, milk
	cheese sandwich, orange juice
	baked chicken, rice, carrots
Thursday	cream of wheat, egg, juice
	chicken sandwich, raisins, milk
	leftover meatloaf, applesauce, yogurt
Friday	cheese toast, peaches
	peanut butter and banana sandwich, milk
	go to Sunday School dinner
Saturday	oatmeal, raisins, milk
	egg sandwich, applesauce, yogurt
	go to Martha's home for dinner with kids
Sunday	cottage cheese, banana, toast
	leftover spaghetti, green peas, bread
	hamburger patty, bread, broccoli, milk

If your parent cannot keep such a chart to ensure healthful nutrition, you may need to get more assistance to be sure the food is being eaten. This menu is only a suggestion. Check with your parent's doctor for specific dietary and liquid requirements that meet their special health needs.

PREVENT A CONFUSED DEMEANOR

Look for a medical problem when there is a change in demeanor. For example, even a relatively minor infection such as a bladder or kidney infection, bronchitis, or pneumonia may create confusion in the elderly. But this confusion may improve and disappear when the infection is discovered and treated. Many other medical problems may aggravate confusion and may be treatable.

Other common causes of increasing confusion include medications, especially those used to aid in sleep and to relieve pain. Because so many types might cause confusion, check the list of medications with your parent's doctor to be sure your parent's confusion is not simply due to a particular medication.

- If no medical problems are causing the confused demeanor, healthful nutrition, including drinking adequate liquids each day, is vital for alertness and mental stamina. If you find that using the suggested charts work for your family, go with this method. But if your parent is unable or unwilling to checkmark the chart on the appropriate day, it may be time to discuss home care.

- A large calendar with activities written in for each week helps to keep your parent oriented as to what events are going on each day.

- Maintaining a schedule each day is very helpful. Challenge your parent to get up at 7:30 A.M., have breakfast at 8:00 A.M., then exercise, and take a bath. If she sleeps until noon, this may add to her confusion.

- Interruptions in the sleep pattern may contribute to your parent being less alert during daytime hours. These interruptions may occur often during the night with your elderly parent. And the more interruptions during the night, the more drowsy your parent will feel during the day making the parent nap frequently, thus starting that vicious cycle of daytime naps and nighttime insomnia. If your parent is experiencing nighttime insomnia, contact her physician for suggestions in how to get restful, uninterrupted sleep and follow the suggestions until you find she is more alert.

PREVENT POOR HOUSEKEEPING

An apparent sudden change in housekeeping cleanliness may be a sign of a medical problem such as depression. Has the vision changed enough to make the tasks more difficult? Has fatigue from improper eating habits limited the physical activity needed for housework? Other medical problems should be ruled out just in case there is a treatable cause of this important change.

- Housekeeping, including maintenance of the home can present a problem for elderly adults. If your parent has not kept up with housekeeping responsibilities, evaluate whether the problem is disorganization or physical difficulties. If you find your parent has no medical problems but is getting weaker with aging, seek outside assistance for those chores that are too difficult. If your parent is disorganized, it is time for a chart.

	M	T	W	T	F	S	S
LAUNDRY							
CHANGE LINENS							
VACUUM							
MOP							
LAWN CARE							
BATHROOMS							
DUST							

Let this chart remind your parent to do one chore every day. If the situation does not improve, seek assistance with a home assistant, companion, lawn service, or chore service, or ask family members to pitch in.

- Ask your parent's physician for a home health evaluation. Ask if an occupational therapist could teach your parent how to efficiently do his daily tasks and learn to use the assistive devices necessary for independence. Evaluating the home as well as the patient can help correct problem areas.

- A physical therapist (PT) could also be requested by the home health nurse or your parent's physician. The PT could help your parent with strength and endurance, which would allow him to do more tasks around his home.

- If you find rotten or spoiled food in the refrigerator, seek support from different family members. Ask siblings or grandchildren to take grocery duty one week a month. This would involve shopping, disinfecting the refrigerator and kitchen, and meal preparation, if needed. If you are the only caregiver and cannot get support from other relatives, friends, or church members, then you may want to hire someone to make sure nutritious food is available and eaten.

PREVENT LACK OF MEDICATION

Some medications are needed to control medical problems and allow normal activity. If you find that your parent's medications are not being taken properly, be sure to rule out any possible treatable medical problem. For example, has memory changed due to an unnoticed stroke? Has a new medical problem such as depression developed?

This problem is a concern to many adult children and physicians who treat the elderly. Taking medicine as prescribed is critical to the health of your parent. If you feel comfortable that your parent has the medications prescribed by his physician but is just forgetful about taking it, then you can easily solve this dilemma. But if you aren't sure your parent has even gotten the prescriptions filled, you must intervene. If your parent will only take medication if someone gives it to him, consider hiring a certified nurse's aid.

- Talk with the physician and know the medication your parent is to take, including the exact doses. When these are called to the pharmacy, be sure to ask for easy-to-open caps if your parent has trouble with his grip. Once these arrive, talk with your parent about daily medication.

- Purchase a pill calendar for your parent. This plastic container has days of the week listed and is divided into parts of the day. It is available at most larger pharmacies. Have someone fill the pill calendar either once a week or once a month, depending on the need.

- If you come over once a week or more often or live out of town and write your parent, send index cards or postcards to put by her medicine. This may be a funny reminder, love note, or something else to get her attention. One woman took a photograph of herself while holding a medication container and pointing to it. She said that her mother thought this was so funny, she taped it on her kitchen cupboard and never forgot to take her medications. Remember, taking too much or too little medication could mean a rapid decline for the parent or even hospitalization.

- If your parent is having trouble reading the prescription due to poor vision, see an ophthalmologist.

- Keep a list with your parent's physician's number, the pharmacist's number, and all medicines and doses by your phone, as well as in your parent's purse or wallet. This information can save time and lives in case too much medication is taken or none is taken at all.

- Make sure your parent's primary physician has a current list of all medications your parent takes, in case of adverse effects. When a new medicine is added, ask questions, and understand the side effects. Ask if the medicine will affect your parent's appetite and how to best take the medicine, with food or on an empty stomach. If a medicine is to be taken at bedtime, put the pill calendar by your parent's nightstand or toothbrush, and if it is to be taken in the morning, put it by the kitchen sink or her placemat at the table.

- If you feel that your parent's medicine isn't doing what it is intended to do, call the physician.

- If your parent cannot be trusted to take the medicine, this is the red flag that more assistance is needed. The parent may need someone to remind him to take the medicine each day or go to his home and give it to him. (Be sure the person you hire is qualified to give medications.)

PREVENT WITHDRAWAL

Many medical problems can contribute to withdrawal, and these might be treatable. Depression is a common cause and can be treated. Embarrassment over incontinence may cause your parent to limit activity and social situations. Chronic pain such as arthritis or back pain is a common but treatable cause of withdrawal from activity. Or perhaps your parent avoids outside or social activities because of difficulty walking.

To keep aging adults from withdrawing from the world around them, an ongoing routine of activity, exercise, and social involvement is needed. Your parent's physician can be sure no other medical problems are present and can make recommendations about the best form of activity and exercise. Challenge your parent to commit to six weeks of activity and exercise. After six weeks, talk with your parent and see how he is feeling. Does he have more or less energy? Is he sleeping better? Does he have less anxiety and a good appetite? See if the benefits of social involvement and exercise are worth it to your parent. Make comments if you have seen some differences in your parent since she started exercising. Does she feel better about herself? Make a chart such as the one shown in chapter 7 if your parent needs a reminder to stay active daily.

- Sometimes a physician will give a patient specific exercises for certain physical problems like back pain, arthritis, incontinence, or osteoporosis. If your parent has been assigned specific exercises, add these to the list of exercises on the chart for variety.

- Social activities are as important to your parent as exercise. If your parent lives alone, plan a social calendar with him. He doesn't have to do something every day, but the chart should list many options. Check with the church, community center, and senior center and see what is going on that might interest your parent to ensure activity during the week.

- If your parent is living with you, motivate him to interact with the family. Your parent can pitch in as part of the family and in so doing feel as if he is part of the family.

• Physical problems like loss of sight or hearing or difficulty walking all require understanding from you and the people your parent socializes with. You can learn more about sensitivity to physical problems of aging in chapter 9.

PREVENT NEGLECTING MAIL AND NEWSPAPER

Just as in other areas of personal care, when mail and newspaper services are neglected, consider the possibility that a medical problem could be contributing. Has a new illness such as dementia begun? Is your parent having trouble walking to get the mail due to back pain or arthritis? Be sure no treatable cause exists. Check with your parent's doctor.

• Some post offices offer a service in which they will call a relative listed on records and let them know the mail is not being picked up.

• So you won't have a buildup of papers in the yard, it may be necessary to cancel the paper for safety purposes.

• Ask a teenager in the neighborhood to pick up the mail and newspaper each afternoon on the way home from school. This also gives you another support service as someone will check on your parent daily and call you if there is no answer.

PREVENT POOR FINANCES

Medical problems such as dementia can change reasoning power and judgment. These commonly cause poor business and financial decisions. Your parent may benefit from medical treatment. Some seemingly unrelated illnesses such as an underactive thyroid may even contribute. Check with your parent's doctor.

If your parent is not capable of taking care of financial affairs, chances are that other problems are being ignored as well.

• If your parent is capable but neglectful, appoint a trusted family member to check with the parent weekly and go over bills due, deposits that need to be made, or any other transactions.

• Have an accountant audit your parent's finances biannually.

What About Communication?

Many elderly adults may experience speech and language problems or disorders for the first time. In some cases, sudden or dramatic changes may occur. In other cases, there is a slow deterioration of language skills over a period of time.

The sudden appearance of a language problem in adults may have several causes. Most of these causes injure the brain in some way. Usually the brain injury is in the left hemisphere of the brain, which is mostly responsible for language functions in a majority of persons. A frequent cause of adult language disorders is a stroke (see chap. 2), which interrupts the flow of blood to various parts of the brain. When brain cells do not receive blood, they may die from lack of oxygen. When the left side of the brain is damaged, adults may suffer a language disorder known as *aphasia*, which is a loss of language. Most aphasic persons do not lose all of their speech and language; the degree of loss varies among individuals. Some aphasic individuals are able to talk fluently, but their speech does not make sense. Most aphasic persons tend to have difficulties in speaking, understanding spoken language, and writing.

Aphasia, therefore, is a breakdown in a person's ability to use and/or to understand language. This breakdown is a result of damage to the brain. Aphasia includes many different types of communication problems and many levels of severity. The family needs to fully understand the communication capabilities of the parent with aphasia. The speech-language pathologist will suggest how the family can best communicate with the aphasic person and how the person can best communicate with the family.

The following suggestions may help you cope with some of the behaviors that are exhibited by a person with aphasia.

- Remember the person is an adult and should always be treated like one. Permit him or her to have as much independence as possible.

- Short range goals, positive reinforcement, and a routine schedule are important.

- Irritability, impulsiveness, and crying or laughing inappropriately may occur because of the brain injury. These behaviors should be ignored as much as possible.

- The person's right or left field of vision may be lost. The person may not respond to people or objects (food, etc.) on that side or field of vision. Always try to approach the person on the unaffected side.

- Speak in simple rather than complex sentences. Use familiar words such as water, bed, chair. Later these nouns could be associated with verbs. For example: eat food, drink water, etc.

- The person may have difficulty saying the names of people or objects. You can help them by making an activity of saying the names of people and objects while the person listens.

- The person may repeat words or actions over and over beyond meaning or when inappropriate. This is known as perseveration and is common in aphasia. When it occurs, change the subject and go on to another topic.

- When asking a question, show the object you are talking about to the person while you are asking the question. Gesturing may also be helpful.

- Be honest and as direct as possible with the person. Develop a "live for today" attitude and praise any signs of progress. Avoid discussions on how long it will take to recover.

Show Empathy: We All Age

No matter how difficult your parent may be or how bizarre her behavior becomes, remember this truth: we will all be old someday! Our societal attitude holds aging as an affliction rather than a natural life change, and this negative view of aging is disastrously reinforced by the media. Articles and advertising never show a mature model, even in displaying fashions designed for women over fifty. A *Newsweek* cover of a sweating, gray-haired young man bears the cover line, "Oh, . . . I'm really turning 50!" Nursing home ads ask: "What shall we do about Mother?" [1]

As we begin to compassionately care for our aging parents, we must understand that old age is not an incurable disease, nor can

---

1. Jere Daniel, "Learning to Love Growing Old," *Psychology Today* (September/ October 1994), 62.

it be solved by spending billions of dollars to mask the signs of aging or to extend our life span.

We should not think or say, "I would never act so moody," or "I could never forget to bathe," or "I would never think of being so rude to someone who cleaned my home." Remember, twenty years ago your parents were in their middle years, right where you are today, and chances are great that they said they would never act like their aging parents. Empathy is vital!

Imagine yourself at age seventy or eighty. What do you see? Is your hair the same color or do you even have hair? What about your senses? Can you still hear or see well? How about your mobility? Are you walking erect or are you having a difficult time getting around with stooped shoulders and aching joints?

To become empathetic to the concerns of aging parents, many hospitals and other care facilities offer sensitivity training. In these programs, participants try special equipment to simulate the problems of aging adults. You will put plugs in your ears and try to hear. You will try to maneuver a wheel chair, a walker, and a cane, while wearing glasses that block your peripheral vision. You may put on sunglasses that have been coated thickly with petroleum jelly, stick cottonballs in your ears, and put on tight gloves to simulate sensitive fingers like in arthritis.

The benefit of a sensitivity course is that once you view the world as your parent does, you will no longer question why an aging adult is tired or cries easily, is unreasonable or irritable, or why she might be fearful even when you know the environment is safe.

YOU CAN DO IT!

By making yourself knowledgeable about your parent's needs and concerns, and weighing these with the information you have, you can make an organized plan for caregiving. Chapters 4 and 5 will list caregiving options along with home care support services. Before you make up your mind about living arrangements, weigh each choice, keep your parent's physical and mental health in mind, and consider your personal and family needs. You can make the right choices with your aging parent so that the caregiving burden is lifted and the beauty of the golden years is enhanced.

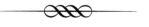

4

THE BENEFITS
OF HOME CARE

"Be it ever so humble, there's no place like home." This song lyric is certainly true for all ages, but perhaps even more so for mature adults. In a recent survey of Americans aged fifty-five or older, 84 percent want to stay in their home as they aged. Maybe this is because there are such positive feelings that all of us associate with being home. Our home is our castle, our refuge from the storm. When we are not feeling well, most of us ask to go home. When we are feeling well, we enjoy the sanctity of our residences and the joy of being with our loved ones.[1]

Ideally, this "aging in place" should be the caregiver's primary choice for an elderly parent as long as the person's needs are being met and as long as home care is adequate and affordable.

Home care refers to the panoply of services provided in the home to help patients stay out of hospitals, nursing homes, and other institutions. Most home care is provided to the frail elderly, but it may also be appropriate for other adults recuperating from accidents or

---

1. *Caring*, vol. IV, no. 10 (October 1985), 12.

illnesses. Family members work with hired personnel to provide certain components of medical and personal home care.[2]

Home care is becoming the "care of choice" for many mature adults. While we have made a great deal of progress in expanding home care services under various federal agencies, we still need better access and greater funding for long-term care. Especially with the aging population in the United States, issues regarding home care will be more prevalent than ever before.

INDEPENDENCE AS A PRIORITY

As we discussed in chapter 3, one of the greatest fears of most elderly persons is of having to leave their homes and give up their independence. *Keeping independence* is the focus of this chapter and should be the joint goal for adult children and their parents as long as possible. To remain in one's home and to live as independently as possible is important. Respecting this goal and looking for creative ways to continue this as your parent ages is optimal.

Now if you think, "Sure, I want my parent to be independent, but she could *never* live alone in her home," you may be surprised. Many elderly adults, even those with physical disabilities, can function well at home. One such person was Debra's grandmother, Nina Holden. Even at age ninety-eight, Nina stayed in her home until a few months before her death. She lived on a central Florida farm, and her oldest daughter, Velma, lived next door (within "hollering" distance, as Velma would say). As Nina's hearing and sight declined, her daughter would stay over at night to make sure she did not fall, and other friends and family would drop in on her during daytime hours to visit. Nina's greatest wish was to remain in her home, and as long as her health allowed it, the family agreed that she would be granted this wish. Staying at home gave her vitality, security, and comfort in her later years.

THE FIRST CHOICE: HOME CARE

The most important reason to allow a parent to live at home is that it is overwhelmingly the desire of most elderly people. And like Velma and her siblings, many adult children can negotiate a

---

2. *The Home Health Handbook* (Pittsburgh: International Masters Publishers, 1993), 5.

way to make it happen. Home care has been a tradition in America for centuries as it keeps families together. Studies show that elderly people who live in their homes heal more quickly from illness; in fact, many studies note that those people who received home care lived longer and had a better quality of life. Even for elderly persons who have terminal illnesses, combining home care with support services such as a hospice enables them to live their days in comfort with support from those who love them most.

This is not to say that living at home will last forever. You must also be prepared for the time when it will be prohibitive for your parent to remain at home, whether for health reasons or for safety or emotional concerns.

A HOME SAFETY REVIEW

As you begin planning for home care, gather family members together and discuss with your parent any concerns about the home situation. Affirm that you want him to stay in his home, but that you want this environment to be safe and healthy. Make sure all siblings agree about home care before this meeting, and use this family time to discuss specific concerns, such as lawn maintenance, housekeeping, or nighttime safety, dividing some responsibilities among able members. Using the checklist below, go over each area of the home during this meeting—indoors and out— to ensure it is safe for elderly adults. Allow your parent to lead the way in this home review, but if they resent your intervention, be firm with your concerns.

Clarice had such a family meeting and sensed animosity from her mother, a newly widowed but independent eighty-three-year-old woman. "As we were going through Mom's home to check for possible problems, I knew that she thought we were intruding. But I was very firm, telling her that we had heard of a number of burglaries in her neighborhood that spring, and her neighborhood was fifty years old; things had changed. We wanted to do everything possible for her to stay in her home as it meant so much to her. But we were also going to make certain that she was safe."

Doing a home safety review with your parent can correct many health and safety problems as you open the lines of communication and show your concern. (See chap. 6 for a full review on home safety.) As you review each of the areas listed below, be sure to write down all observations.

HOME SAFETY REVIEW CHECKLIST

Living Room. Check electrical cords and outlets, frayed rugs, walk-space through room, tile level, slippery wooden floors, proper lighting, step-ups into other rooms, fireplace safety, window locks, door locks, furniture height, and balance and stability.

Bedrooms. Check frayed rugs, bedspreads that are too long, chairs that are unstable, locks on windows, electrical cords and outlets, walk-space, slippery wooden floors, and adequate lighting.

Kitchen. Check hot water temperature, electrical outlets and cords, slippery tile floors, equipment safety (refrigerator, stove, dishwasher), accessibility of food items and canned goods, balanced kitchen table and chairs, gas stove, leaky faucets, and proper lighting.

Bathrooms. Check for slippery floors, nonskid mats in tub and on floor, grab bars by toilet and in bathtub, easy-to-reach shelf for bath products and soaps, nightlights, liquid soaps to avoid slipping on bars, medications on low shelf for easy reach, water temperature at safe level, and leaky faucets.

Hallways. Check for frayed rugs and slippery floors, good lighting, grab bars secured tightly, if needed, and no clutter.

Garage or Carport. Check for slippery floors, equipment that is not stored safely, gasoline or other chemicals that are not closed tightly and placed away from the house, and glass or containers that could drop and break.

Roof. Check for leaks, missing shingles, rotten wood on eaves and awnings, and unsecured bricks in chimney.

Lawn and Property. Check for holes in lawn, sprinkler heads that are not attached, hoses that could trip someone, dead or dying trees, broken limbs and branches, and shrubs covering windows.

GET A HOME HEALTH CARE EVALUATION

The next step is to request a home health care evaluation. This assessment can help rule out some stumbling blocks before they occur as you work toward home care for your parent. Contact your parent's physician's office, the discharge nurse at the hospital, the area agency on aging, a social worker or geriatric care manager, and seek a referral to the proper agency, such as visiting home health nurse.

A visiting nurse will come to your parent's home and assess physical, emotional, and mental strengths and weaknesses. Be sure to ask if Medicare will cover the charge for this evaluation prior to the appointment. It should be covered if it is specifically requested by a medical provider, although the services necessary may not all be covered.

When your parent is evaluated by the visiting nurse, the following areas are usually considered:

- Sight

- Hearing

- Speech

- Communication

- Mental and behavior status

- Skin condition

- Dressing

- Toileting

- Ambulation

- Transfer

- Wheel chair use

- Bladder control

- Bowel control

- Bathing

- Feeding

- Endurance

Each area evaluated is rated, such as:

- Sight:

(1) Good
(2) Vision adequate—unable to read/see details
(3) Vision limited—gross object differentiation
(4) Blind

- Ambulation:

(1) Independence with/without assistive device
(2) Walks with supervision
(3) Walks with continuous human support
(4) Bed to chair (total help)
(5) Bedfast

- Bladder control:

(1) Continence
(2) Rarely incontinent
(3) Occasional—once/week or less
(4) Frequent—up to once a day
(5) Total incontinence
(6) Catheter—indwelling

Once the home health evaluation is complete, the physician must sign the form before recommended services can be given.

CONTACT THE POLICE AND FIRE DEPARTMENTS

Ask the local fire department to make an inspection for fire hazards at your parent's home. They will point out changes that need to be made, including necessary safety equipment such as smoke alarms, fire alarms, and a fire extinguisher, and will show you how to plan for evacuation, in case of fire. Also, upon request, the police department will send a representative to talk about home safety and to make sure your parent's home is secure from theft. It is a good time to let both agencies know that your parent lives alone.

MAKE NECESSARY IMPROVEMENTS

When you have carefully evaluated your parent's personal needs and home condition, discuss the observations together. Talk about areas that need changing, such as new dead-bolt locks on doors for added safety or an alarm system connected to local police and rescue units or an Emergency Response System (see chap. 6). Discuss health problems that could prevent your parent from quality living at home, such as special dietary needs for the diabetic or the demands of a two-story home for the person with chronic back pain, arthritis, or a heart condition. Perhaps ramps and other accommodations need to be made for a wheelchair. Decide how to address these needs that would give everyone involved peace of mind yet still allow for the much-needed independence.

Sam did a home safety review for his elderly mother who lived alone and suffered from arthritis. "My brother and I inspected every inch of her home last summer," he said. "We checked the entry, the lighting, the kitchen area, the bathroom, bedroom, and living area and found many places where improvements for safety were needed. The doors and windows lacked security, the lighting at entries of her home was too dim, the accessibility of cabinet items in the kitchen was too high for Mom to reach easily, and even the bathroom was dangerous with slippery tile."

Sam had a security system put in that was connected to emergency medical services, the police, and the fire department with an emergency response button if his mother felt afraid or could not get to the phone. He added higher voltage lights to both entry ways, and reminded his mom to leave these on at night. With suggestions from an occupational therapist referred by her physician, Sam rearranged the kitchen cabinets so that the items used most often were placed in lower cabinets. The bathroom was made safer with skid proof mats in the tub, grab bars attached to the wall, and a stool secured in the tub to sit on while bathing. He even attached a large sheet of poster board to the wall by her telephone, and in large print, he wrote emergency phone numbers.

The end result? His mother felt comfortable that her home was more secure, and Sam and his brother felt confident that she was safer while still being independent and living at home.

MAKE JOINT DECISIONS, IF POSSIBLE

Include your parent in the decision-making as you decide where changes must be made for personal safety. If you make the decisions together, compliance will be easier. If your parent becomes angry with your involvement, remind him that in order to stay in his home, some changes are necessary for personal safety.

This is where balance is so important. We discussed being "good enough" in chapter 1, and again being "good enough" will play a key role in your negotiation on home safety. When Ted expressed tremendous concern over his spry seventy-eight-year-old father living alone, he had to accept "good enough."

"My dad knows no limits," Ted told us. "He is a diabetic and takes insulin, and I have a home health nurse check on him three times a week. Other than that, he is ready to go!

"I can drive up to visit him, and there he is with the weedeater, trying to mow the grass on the side of the hill next to the lake. Of course, he'll wave, claiming everything's fine. Sometimes I think I'm going to have a heart attack just worrying about what Dad will do next."

For peace of mind, Ted had to learn how to firmly put some limits on his father, but allow his father to make choices within these limits. "I told him that I knew he enjoyed exercise and activity, but he had to stop using heavy equipment when no one was home to help him. He absolutely did not want to hear that, but he realized how worried I was and finally agreed. I still get phone calls from his neighbors that he goes out and trims his hedges with clippers when I leave, but he does not weedeat down steep hills or mow the lawn."

While Ted did not take away all of his father's freedom, he did give safety suggestions and set limits about what was no longer acceptable. While the situation was not perfect as far as Ted or his father was concerned, it was "good enough" for both to live with.

SEEKING SUPPORT HELP FOR HOME CARE

When looking for support services for home care, keep in mind that you want to maximize what your parent can do and minimize any assistance. In other words, focus on your parent's strengths so she can stay active in life instead of dwelling on what she cannot do. If you provide help for tasks that he is still able to do, you virtually rob him of his independence. When aging adults lose their independence, you can count on a decline in physical effort and mental alertness.

If your parent can load the dishwasher after meals, encourage this. Perhaps he can take the garbage out or sweep the driveway or clean the bathroom. If she is bedridden due to illness but can sit up and use her arms, let her fold her laundry, snap the green beans for dinner, put old pictures in an album, or feed a grandbaby. When the elderly stop being a part of their environment, they give up on life. If they can feel that their contribution to life is important, their mental outlook will stay positive. And a positive mental outlook is the key for good health and quality of life. The side benefit for involving aging parents in tasks according to their physical ability is that such tasks use the parent's range of motion, helping to keep them limber and active.

If your parent does need some assistance, you have many choices. By having home care you can greatly reduce the responsibility you have to do physical chores for your parent, leaving your energy for the emotional and psychological needs. Carefully select these support services to balance your parent's needs, keeping in mind the costs involved.

When choosing support services for home care, the following are some questions you might ask:

- What physical limitation(s) does my parent have?
- What special needs do I notice?
- What special needs does my parent speak of?
- Is transportation necessary for this support service?
- Who will pay for the home care?
- Who will check to make sure the service was performed?
- Does my parent have special emotional requirements that would hinder this home care?
- Are there any barriers that might occur when someone comes to his home (alarm systems, unfriendly animals, uninformed or suspicious neighbors)?
- How long will the home care services be required?
- Can we cancel the services at any time if dissatisfied?
- Are there contracts that must be signed?
- Must we pay any money upfront for services?

Once you have established your parent's specific needs, look through the following preferred home care services for the elderly. Depending on the size and demand of your community, this list may differ. Find out what is available and how to apply for immediate assistance.

ADULT DAY CARE

There are a reported three thousand adult day care centers in the United States today. While this number seems high, it is not nearly enough to meet the population needs. Adult day care is a safe alternative to nursing home care and costs an average of thirty to forty dollars a day or less, depending on the person's ability to pay, and is usually free for indigents. This program is designed to provide respite for the caregiver during daytime hours. The care can be strictly social and nonmedical, or it can provide medical services.

The *social nonmedical program* provides supervised activities, nutritious meals and snacks, and a place to nap and relax while the elderly spend time with senior friends and staff. The *medical day care* provides the same social environment yet includes medical assistance as needed. Staff members at the medical adult day care are qualified to take blood pressure, give medication, monitor acute and chronic medical problems, and perhaps even work with Alzheimer's patients. Certified staff members at many adult day care centers offer physical therapy, occupational therapy, and speech therapy. Check your senior listings or area agency on aging to see what is available that will meet your parent's needs.

The group setting of the adult day care encourages senior adults to socialize with others. Your physician and social services can develop a treatment plan for your parent's specific needs. By involving your parent in a program that offers social and rehabilitative services, you will help improve his level of activity and prevent decline.

AREA AGENCY ON AGING

The Area Agency on Aging is listed in your phone book. This federally funded agency provides services for those aged sixty and older and is an important starting place as you look for home care services. You will receive advice on how to obtain services such as personal care, friendly visitors, nutritious meals, chore service, transportation, and homemaker assistance. These professionals are trained to help you with referrals and problem-solving involving the elderly.

Describe your parent's situation, and ask if you could have a counselor or social worker come and evaluate her situation. The social worker will tell you what funded home care your parent qualifies for and what care is available in the community that you can supplement. You may need to go to the agency and fill out paper work before a home evaluation can be done. If your parent does not qualify or if there is a waiting list, ask for suggestions and names of reliable organizations that also give respite and support services.

CHORE SERVICE

This housekeeping service helps to maintain the home for those who are physically limited. It can include any service that helps keep the home clean, from vacuuming, mopping, and cleaning windows to cleaning ovens and woodwork or even making small repairs. You may call independent cleaning services in your yellow pages or ask about such at your Area Agency on Aging. If you hire a housekeeping service, be sure that it is bonded and insured. If you personally hire someone to do chores through an advertisement, do a thorough background and reference check. You may call an area church to see if any groups provide this service. Often church youth groups will do a monthly chore service for shut-ins for a small donation to their program.

EMERGENCY RESPONSE SYSTEM

This system allows your parent to notify ERS of a problem if he cannot get to the phone. The Area Agency on Aging will know what systems are available in your community. As a community outreach, the systems can be rented for as low as twenty-five dollars per month with no charge for calls. Some organizations offer subsidized placement of the system to seniors who cannot afford this service.

Most systems require the person to press a button on the machine each morning when he gets up and then again at bedtime. This signal means that all is well. If the person fails to press the button one morning or evening (every twelve hours), the monitoring company will call the home. If there is no answer, the company will call the emergency contact number listed (usually the adult child or a neighbor). If this contact does not answer, the monitoring company will call the police and have the situation checked out. If the person goes on vacation, the button can be deactivated. Besides the monitoring system, a special necklace with a button is worn by the person so if he falls or cannot get to a phone, he can push the panic button to start the system.

An emergency response system can offer peace of mind if your parent lives alone or far away from you. If you have two parents who are frail or one who is bedridden, the company will give you two necklaces with panic buttons. The bedridden parent can also have a speaker phone installed that allows him to answer the phone without getting up.

FRIENDLY VISITOR/COMPANION

Many different organizations offer this companion service. Your Area Agency on Aging has information on what is available in your community. The friendly visitor or companion is just that—a person who visits your parent to ease the loneliness. This person can read to your parent, help write letters, talk, listen to favorite music, share a meal, go for a walk or out on an outing. Whatever you feel will enhance your parent's life—within limits—can be requested of this companion.

Many churches now provide this type of companion service as an outreach ministry to elderly homebound. Even working members can make a brief visit during evening hours or a daily phone call from the office to the homebound person. In one large church, the youth take on this companion program as a service project during the summer months.

HOMEMAKER ASSISTANT/PERSONAL CAREGIVER

This assistant would help take care of your parent's personal care, such as bathing, toileting, dressing, fixing nutritious meals, doing laundry, running errands, shopping for groceries, providing transportation to appointments, and light housekeeping. If you wish to have medicine given to your parent, be certain the assistant is certified to give medications and is monitored by a nurse or medical provider.

Homemaker assistants can be found through home health care services or you can hire an individual independently. These professional service agencies guarantee trained and bonded assistants and will send a substitute if the employee does not come for some reason. While hiring a homemaker assistant through a service generally costs more than hiring someone personally, you will have peace of mind knowing that a qualified individual will be with your parent during required times.

If you plan to hire your own homemaker assistant, ask for referrals from friends, your parent's physician, the pastor, or church members. Explain the necessary duties and be honest with what you intend to pay. Some people run classified advertisements in the local paper or put up notices at a nearby junior college or university, as many college students have flexible hours and need extra income. Get references, and follow up on these no matter how qualified the applicant seems. If they will be driving your parent to appointments or shopping, be sure to get an address, phone number, driver's license number, automobile insurance number, social security number, and student ID, if in college.

HOME MAINTENANCE AND REPAIR

Maintenance and repair programs for senior citizens are offered by many states. Plumbers, carpenters, painters, electricians, and other professionals are available to assist senior citizens with home repairs, if they qualify. Check with your Area Agency on Aging to see what is offered in your area.

HOME WEATHERIZATION PROGRAM AND UTILITY BILL ASSISTANCE

Programs that assist eligible individuals in weatherizing their home are available for seniors. These state or federally funded programs provide services such as caulking, insulating, and weather stripping. A federally funded program called Low Income Home Energy Assistance Program (LIHEAP) offers utility assistance programs for seniors who meet certain criteria. These programs are usually available for renters as well as homeowners. Check with your Area Agency on Aging for a referral to the proper organization for help.

LAWN SERVICE

Chances are that you will need to hire someone to help with your parent's lawn upkeep. Landscaping services are available through the Yellow Pages that will make sure the lawn and shrubs stay in good condition. Usually these services bill you monthly. You may also find a neighbor who would like to make extra money and would be willing to maintain your parent's property. The only drawback in hiring someone privately is the liability involved. Lawn services carry separate insurance policies in case of injury; a neighbor who is injured on your parent's property would not have a separate policy, and your parent would be responsible. Get references if you do not know the individual.

LEGAL AID

Contact the local bar association for a referral. They will let you know which attorneys are familiar with legal concerns of the elderly and provide you with fee information, depending on your parent's income.

LOCAL RED CROSS

The Red Cross has been a senior advocate for decades. Some chapters offer a layman's basic home nursing course to help you learn to care for your parent if ill; some offer transportation to and from the doctor. The Red Cross CPR course is excellent. Call your local chapter to see what services are available.

MAIL CHECK

Your local postmaster may offer a program that will provide notification if your parent does not pick up mail one day. This is another safety check, especially for out-of-town adult children.

MEAL PLAN

If you fear that your parent is not eating properly and does not care to join one of the meal plans suggested, you can initiate your own meal plan using a favorite restaurant. Call ahead once a week, and order seven meals (per parent) from this restaurant. Have the restaurant box these up so they can be frozen, label the contents, then arrange to pick these up at a certain time. Your parent can take out one meal each day, microwave, and add a salad or fruit for a balanced, nutritious meal. If you are long distance caregiving, see if a neighbor or friend would do this service for a small fee. Some churches provide a similar service by freezing meals for the elderly when they have church night suppers and delivering these to homebound individuals.

NUTRITIOUS MEALS

Nutritious meals are provided by many organizations services, depending on the size and demand of the community. Meals on Wheels is currently the main organization across the nation and maintains a strong reputation for providing reasonable and nutritious meals for the elderly. If your parent can get the service, it usually is provided five to seven days per week. This includes one hot meal and sometimes a cold meal delivered at the same time, at an average cost of four dollars per meal, depending on income level. This reflects what is typically provided, but every community is different. You can check your phone book under Meals on Wheels, Area Agency on Aging, senior services, or call area churches for referrals.

REASSURANCE CALLS

These telephone calls are made to your parent as often as necessary, usually once a day at the same time. The reassurance call should include a friendly conversation and also a personal check to ensure your parent's well-being. If the parent does not answer the phone, the caller is instructed to call the designated person on your parent's card and let that person know that there is no answer. Because the homebound person usually looks forward to the reassurance call, no answer is a red flag for someone to go to the home and make a personal check.

Often volunteers at a community center or church do reassurance calls as a service or for donations to their cause. If your parent's church does not provide this kind of outreach, it is worth pursuing as even elderly members can provide this service out of their home and feel benevolent.

RESPITE CARE

This care is given to your parent while you are away. It may be for as few as several hours or all day depending on the need. This person would stay with your parent and be the responsible caregiver in your absence, making necessary decisions as directed. The Area Agency on Aging has more information about respite care with lists of persons who are available and fee information. Many churches also are becoming actively involved in this volunteer service.

RETIRED SENIOR VOLUNTEERING PROGRAM

Retired Senior Volunteering Program (RSVP) is an organization of retired volunteers. Check with your Area Agency on Aging to see if you have a chapter in your community. RSVP is a great resource of services and also a great place for seniors to volunteer in their area of interest. Retired professionals such as CPAs, attorneys, teachers, and others offer their expertise and knowledge. Depending on your parent's health and mobility, they could benefit by volunteering with RSVP or as a recipient of these services.

SENIOR CENTERS

Senior centers can provide an array of services, including social interaction, physical activity, educational programs, nutritious meals, field trips and more. Look under senior citizens' service organizations in the Yellow Pages or check with local churches near your parent's home.

TRANSPORTATION/ESCORT SERVICES

Transportation is available from various sources—through homemaker's assistants, the Red Cross, local churches, senior organizations, private agencies, and more. Taxi companies often give senior citizens discounted fares. Escort services can meet the need of the frail elderly by going with them to their appointment or assisting with shopping and errands. Your Area Agency on Aging is a beginning resource for a listing of providers of transportation.

WORKING SENIORS

This program is designed to help those over fifty-five in finding a job. Usually the job is part-time, with the typical minimum of fifteen hours per week. Your Area Agency on Aging can refer you to a working seniors' program if your parent needs or wants to work.

WORKING WITH HOME CARE SERVICES

Before you begin spending money on home care support services, ask your parent's physician if any of these services are covered under government assistance, either Medicare, Medicaid or other senior programs. Care such as transportation, homemaker assistance or respite care is often funded by government agencies (Area Agency on Aging), if your parent qualifies. It is best to ask these questions beforehand, fill out the appropriate forms, and allow Medicaid or Medicare to pay for home care services before you begin paying.

YOUR PARENT'S RIGHTS

Your parent has the right to be treated with dignity and respect by anyone who enters her home. Remember, the home care agency is working for your parent— so do not hesitate to ask for a change if either of you are not satisfied with the personnel assigned to the case. Be certain the agency has a twenty-four-hour emergency number. [3]

TIPS FOR TIGHT BUDGETS

If you are not having luck receiving funded services for home care, here are a few tips to tighten your budget yet still receive the help your parent needs:

- Let the professionals know that your parent's budget is tight; ask if they will accept assignment or give a reduction in price.

- Seek help from benevolent agencies such as local churches or community organizations. Many times these volunteers will offer free or discounted services to those elderly in need.

- Interview neighbors who are retired and have free time. Offer to pay for their part-time services—to get your parent's mail, mow their lawn, check on them daily or make an evening phone call, take your parent to the grocery store or doctors' appointments.

- Hire a responsible teenager to do lawn care or clean your parent's home weekly, pick up the mail, collect newspapers, and more.

- Divide the responsibilities between siblings, grandchildren, and cousins—anyone who lives in town. If each person took

---

3. *The Home Health Handbook*, 5.

several days a month to check on aging parents, your problems and anxiety will be reduced (see sample home care schedule below).

- Look into trading "adult sitting" with friends in the same situation. For example, you can take care of your friend's mom, and she can reciprocate by looking after yours. This may be for one day a week or it could allow each of you to take much-needed family vacations. This also encourages socialization for your parent as he is "forced" to be with another adult.

- Consider starting a social adult day care in your church one or more mornings a week. This is similar to a Mother's Morning Out program that churches have for young children. A group of volunteers will plan the activities, chaperone field trips, provide food and more, and a small fee is charged to cover expenses.

- Start a noon meal program at your church for seniors in your community.

HOME CARE SCHEDULE

If your budget is tight, a home care schedule could make all the difference. Make a schedule similar to the one printed. At a family meeting, delegate various responsibilities and have the persons fill in the blanks for a month at a time (the sample is for two weeks). Each person should check his or her name as the duty is completed. This will ensure that your parent receives on-going care.

Sample Home Care Schedule for Mrs. Jones

Date	Responsibility	Designated Person
May		
1	Weekly housekeeping	Martha and Rick
2	Bring 7 frozen meals	Martha
3	Lawn mowing	Pete (neighbor)
4	Phone call	Sandra (neighbor)
5	Home visit	Visiting nurse

Sample Home Care Schedule for Mrs. Jones (Continued)

Date	Responsibility	Designated Person
6	Phone call	Sandra (neighbor)
7	Grocery store/Dr. appt.	Karen
8	Weekly housekeeping	Joe and Patty
9	Bring 7 frozen meals	Sunday school class
10	Lawn mowing	Pete (neighbor)
11	Phone call	Sandra (neighbor)
12	Home visit	Visiting nurse
13	Phone Call	Sandra (neighbor)
14	Grocery store/Dr. appt.	Karen

For the Jones family, this schedule works great. Martha and Patty, Mrs. Jones's daughters, take care of housekeeping and meals along with their husbands, Rick and Joe. The visiting nurse was requested by Mrs. Jones's physician and stops by each week to check her blood pressure and blood sugar level. Karen, Patty's college-age daughter, enjoys taking her grandmother shopping and to appointments on Friday mornings. Pete, a fifteen-year-old neighbor who is saving for a car, is responsible enough to handle the lawn mowing each week. Mrs. Jones pays for this service monthly out of her social security check. Sandra, Mrs. Jones's retired neighbor, accepts no payment and volunteers to call her friend several times a week to check on her "because I enjoy doing this." And the Sunday School class volunteers take turns bringing home-cooked meals and visiting with Mrs. Jones.

This type of home care costs virtually pennies and can be organized by any family with great caregiving needs but a tight budget. Many people are willing to help a little, and if everyone pitches in, it adds up to quality, loving care.

HOME CARE AFTER HOSPITALIZATION

Home care after hospitalization is becoming more popular, especially with patients who do not require constant medical monitoring.

When your parent is about to be released from the hospital or a nursing home, a discharge team will make a recommendation for home care. In most cases, the hospital will send a home health nurse to your parent's home, or make an evaluation before you leave for home, if this is recommended by your physician. Medicare should cover this expense. If you choose to use the home health care from your hospital, the transition should be fairly easy as the hospital will have your parent's medical information readily available.

We listed some available services earlier in this chapter. If your parent requires a service by a certified provider, Medicare will cover the allowable fees if it is recommended by a physician.

SEEK INFORMATION

Meet with the social worker(s) in charge of your parent's case, and get all the information on the discharge plan (see sample questions below). Learn how to take care of any medical problem your parent has, such as how to dress a wound, monitor blood sugar levels, or give ongoing medication. Sometimes members of the hospital staff will assume that you know more than you do because they are used to the procedures. Ask questions until you feel comfortable with the new situation. Also ask the social worker or discharge nurse what medical equipment will be furnished to make your parent's recovery at home easier. If recommended by the physician, some equipment can be sent to your home to make the transition easier until your parent is well. Ask if these items will be ordered and if they will be covered by Medicare. You may be able to get a walker, wheel chair, oxygen equipment, hospital bed, or even a bedside commode.

ASK QUESTIONS

Knowledge is the key to a comfortable transition as you bring your parent home from hospitalization or a stay in a nursing home.

The following represent some pertinent questions you can ask the discharge team:

- What are the medications needed, including the doses and time of dose? What side effects should these have? What side effects are not normal? Should these be taken with food or not?

- Am I to assist with any procedures such as changing dressings, assisting with range of motion exercises, or others?

- What daily living tasks are allowed (bathing, dressing, walking to table, feeding self, walking to bathroom or using bedside commode or bed pan)? If they are not allowed at present, when can these tasks be added?

- What home health care assistance is available and provided upon release from the hospital?

- What are the specific services provided? (Obtain a detailed list of services, such as personal care, medication, meals, therapy, etc.)

- How long is my parent covered through Medicare for home health services?

- How much will we have to pay as long as Medicare is covering the home health care?

- How often will the home care personnel come? Can they start right away?

- Does Medicare cover any equipment? Does it cover a wheelchair, bedside commode, walker, or hospital bed?

- If Medicare does cover equipment, will the discharge team ask the doctor to order this?

- Who will be in charge of my parent's case?

- Which physician will be in direct communication with the home health service? (Usually there are several on consult at the hospital.)

- How much notice will I have when the home care services are no longer covered by Medicare?

- How do I know if my parent is covered by Medicaid? Whom do I call to receive information?

- Is physical therapy, occupational therapy, or speech therapy covered at home for my parent under Medicare?

- What do we do when these services are no longer covered?

- Does the discharge team ask for these services as well? If not, which therapist would you recommend?

- Will supplemental insurance policies cover extra expenses?

- Whom do we call in case of medical emergency? With whom would we speak to ask general questions? What would be considered an emergency for my parent's condition?

- Do we need a geriatric care manager to handle this case? Whom would you recommend? How much does it cost? Is the cost covered by any insurance?

These represent basic questions. You should add to the list specific concerns regarding your parent's situation. The discharge team members are experts in this area and are willing to answer all of your questions—that is their primary duty.

When your parent is covered for home care after a stay in the hospital or nursing home, a nurse or social worker will follow the case and manage the services. When your parent is no longer able to receive this assistance, it may be time to get an evaluation for future home care.

CHART YOUR PARENT'S PROGRESS

Prepare a chart of your parent's progress each day until the final release by the doctor. Then if your parent has a relapse, the chart provides necessary information for medical professionals to respond quickly and knowledgeably.

On the chart, write down the date, time, and behavior each day, such as:

Tuesday:	Dad had no appetite all day and only drank 2 cups of liquid. He seemed very depressed and slept most of the day.
Wednesday:	At 9 A.M., Dad seemed very weak when trying to sit up. He ate some breakfast but ate an ample lunch. At 5 P.M. Dad was able to walk from the bed to the kitchen for dinner.
Thursday:	Dad had a low grade fever all night. He seemed sore from walking, but he wanted to try again. Appetite has increased, and he is drinking more liquid.

This chart will let the physician know if the patient needs immediate attention or if he is progressing well at home.

Help Acclimate the Patient to the Environment

If your parent is moving into your home or coming home to his own home but still need care while recuperating, it is wise to prepare the room and bed for the bedridden patient. Give your parent a centrally located room. You will need to prepare the room ahead of discharge for your parent's specific needs. Some helpful suggestions for a bedridden elderly person include the following:

- Rent a hospital bed with a pullup bar. Be sure to check with the discharge team to see if this is covered by Medicare.

- Place a plastic pillow cover over your parent's pillow to protect it from the sweating of a fever, spitting up, or spills.

- Put a plastic sheet under their sheet for protection.

- Have several pillows available to prop behind your parent when sitting up.

- Have available several gowns, pajama sets, and robes for needed changes along with additional sets of undergarments.

- Have a lightweight cover in case your parent is chilled.

- Have a bedside table with a bell to ring for assistance.

- Have a pad of paper (to record your parent's progress as well as medication taken and side effects), make up, mirror, hairbrush, toothbrush and paste or mouth swabs (if mouth has sores), a denture dish, handy wipes, facial tissues, a radio, or any other small items that might be needed.

- Have a pitcher filled with fresh water and a plastic cup.

- Provide paper cups to spit into after brushing teeth.

- Provide an activity basket or box filled with reading glasses, Bible, devotional material, magazines, lightweight books, newspapers, crossword puzzles, TV channel changer, paper and pens, envelopes, address book, note cards, stamps, etc.

- Have bathing supplies next to the bed, including a bedside basin to wash hair in. These can be purchased from a medical supply store. Or a child's raft can be used with the hollow center holding water, or a regular raft can be inflated part of the way for the head to lay on. You should add only enough water to wet and rinse the hair. You may want to have two water basins (one for clean water and one for soapy water). Have two washcloths and towels (one under the patient; one to dry), two hand towels to cover patient while bathing for privacy, shampoo, soap, deodorant, tooth brush or mouth swabs, toothpaste, baby oil (if parent has dry skin, you can dry the patient off with a wet washcloth soaked in a moisturizer), and hairbrush.

- Always have toilet supplies nearby with a bedpan and urinal, toilet tissue, tongs for wiping (if it is difficult for parent), handy wipes, and a bedside commode. Check with the discharge team and see if Medicare will cover the rental when your parent comes home from the hospital.

- If your parent requires special equipment such as a wheel chair, walker, or cane, have these available.

USE THE GERIATRIC CARE MANAGER

As described earlier, a geriatric care manager is most helpful to coordinate several home care services. When you are talking to a case manager about your parent, be sure to inquire about personal training, experience, and references. Is the agency bonded? How does the agency secure services? How are the workers trained and supervised? Someone who works with the frail elderly and is aware of potential fraud will understand your concerns. If they seem hesitant to provide background information, call someone else.

When you meet with the case manager, be sure your parent is included in the conversation and not "talked about." Make certain the case manager shows respect to your parent and that your parent feels comfortable with this person.

A case manager can pull resources from a variety of places. Some services will be free and the cost of some depend on the financial status of the parent. Your case manager will know what is available according to that information.

If you get your evaluation through the Area Agency on Aging, the charges are on a sliding scale according to what your parent's income is. Always ask about charges and arrange payment before the service is started.

The Option of Home-Sharing

Home-sharing is a concept that allows your parent to stay in his home and share expenses with a boarder or provide a room for someone in exchange for services. How they do this depends on what would meet your parent's need the most. Check with your pastor, neighbors, friends, and relatives, and see if there is someone they know who would be interested in this type of living arrangement. Always be sure to get many references and follow up on them.

The Importance of Contracts. Make certain the responsibilities for the boarder are carefully outlined in writing, if it is not a room rental. Determine the services expected, frequency of services, days off, holidays, and more. Outline on paper what the renter will receive for such services. If this is a rental agreement, have a contract signed along with an escape clause for both parties. Be very clear on what is expected as far as privacy, food, music, smoking, alcohol, outside visitors, and any other important issues.

The Long Distance Caregiver

Perhaps the most difficult situation with aging parents is when you live far away, and your parent needs constant care. You have responsibilities to your own family and your career, and it is difficult to drop everything and run to your parent's side when frequent problems arise. Yet, what if you are the only one your parent can rely on?

Some adult children cannot take the long distance worries, so they pack up the parent (sometimes against his wishes), moving him to their home. Others move a parent into a facility in his or her own town. A viable option is to see what is available in community services, home care, and private care in your parent's town. Making the choice of home care could allow your parent to adjust slowly to the fact that leaving the home might be necessary in the future. Let your parent know that you will try the home care as long as you can work out a safe and healthy situation in the parent's home, but if this does not work, other options for living arrangements will have to be discussed. The line of communication is then open for change.

This chapter on home care has presented the ideal situation. Home care allows aging parents to continue their independence with services to meet their special needs. As you may have experienced, there may come a time when home care is no longer a reality, and the parent must move in with adult children or go to a retirement center or to a nursing care facility. When do you make this choice? How do you know which is best for the parent's needs? Who is affected? How will it be paid for?

Chapter 5 will address all of these concerns as we list more caregiving options you can make when home care no longer works.

5

LONG-TERM CARE: WHAT YOU MUST KNOW

"It all started with that phone call last summer," Judy, a full-time secretary and the mother of young adults, told us. "My eighty-seven-year-old mother had been living alone since Dad died nine years ago. But one morning while I was at work, Mom called the office and was very upset. She said that she could not live alone any more. She was so distraught that I left the office and rushed to her home. When I walked in, she seemed so fragile and confused. I packed an overnight bag then took her to my home, and she has been living here ever since."

The startling phone call—you may understand what this means. When you experience one emergency call from an ill or frightened parent, you begin to anticipate that more will follow . . . and often they do. For parents who have been fortunate enough to live independently in their home, that phone call also signals their need for support; it becomes a connecting link from adult autonomy to a new dependence on adult children.

GROWTH OF THE POPULATION NEEDING CARE

According to the latest U.S. Census Bureau reports, Americans eighty-five and older represent 1.2 percent of the population and are the fastest growing group, as well as the poorest and sickest. This percentage represents three million Americans who are eighty-five and older, an astounding increase of 232 percent since 1960, with predicted increases of six million people over eighty-five by 2020 and 15 million by 2050. Of this number, many elderly adults need constant care but cannot pay for it. Of this oldest age group, one in four lives in a nursing home.

Typically, the oldest population, like Judy's mother, depends on alternate care such as living with adult children, nursing homes, retirement villages, foster homes, or congregate housing, and this population grows larger each day.

PLANNING FOR LONG-TERM CARE

No one is ever ready when parents reach the stage of requiring long-term care. Because the population is living longer than ever before, adult children must know that long-term care is a reality and be prepared to face this challenge.

This care will include a variety of services, including medical, social and personal care for a chronically ill or disabled parent. But, as you understand the available choices and resources, you can make educated and reasonable decisions when the time comes.

PREPARE FINANCIALLY

No one plans on a long, lingering illness, but it is important to discuss ahead of time what resources your parent has to pay for an illness that mandates long-term care. Learn what services are covered by Medicare, Medicaid, and supplemental insurance policies your parent may have. Medigap and supplemental Medicare coverage generally do not cover long-term care (see chap. 10 for an in-depth discussion on long-term care insurance).

EVALUATE TYPES OF CARE

Long-term care does not necessarily mean placement in a nursing home. By looking at all of the available services you may have some time for yourself and your parent before you must make the move to a more restricted environment. As discussed in chapter 3, a geriatric care manager can help you evaluate the different services that are available and how to pay for these. This trained person will tell you what is offered free, what is on a sliding scale according to income, and what must be covered by other sources.

You are going to learn some options other than home care that are available when parents are no longer able to live alone. With your parent's participation, you will learn to evaluate what type of living arrangement is needed, what type of financing this will take, and how to find services that meet their particular needs. As you begin this transition together—adult children and parents—you can adjust to the aging process, thus allowing your parents to go from independence to dependence with respect and dignity— something everyone deserves.

Make a Plan of Action

The first goal for seeking alternate care when a parent cannot live at home is to find the one choice that allows the maximum independence possible. Let your parent participate in this decision-making process to the extent that he is able. If after reading chapter 4 you are unsure if home care is for your parent, read the options in this chapter and see if these fit your situation. It frequently takes a combination of services to meet your parent's special needs, and there are many options available.

The Multigenerational Family Setting

Studies show that as long as home care is possible, most people sixty-five-years of age and older would prefer to get help at home rather than move to a facility. And many people over sixty-five would prefer living in a retirement facility that can meet their needs before moving in with adult children.

When home care is no longer an option for your parent, and if your parent does not choose to live in a retirement complex, you may decide to invite your parent into your own home. A reported one out of six Americans age sixty-five and over lives in a family member's home. The benefit of having the parent live with you is that you can monitor her daily care and still have access to private and public home care support services. This plethora of tools can ensure a safe and healthy situation for your parent, while allowing the most independence possible.

Before you present the possibility of moving to your parent, discuss the advantages and disadvantages with your spouse and children. It is most helpful to get a sheet of paper and write down pros and cons. The outcome will be obvious once you have considered all factors, including your parent's health and safety, the ability to afford residential care, the need for medical care, the communication in your family, your commitment to caregiving, your family's privacy and busy schedule, your children's ages and activities, and more.

After the joint decision has been made to invite parents to live in your home, approach them with this possibility. It is vital that they make the decision agreeably rather than your giving an ultimatum. This move could be a temporary measure, or it could be permanent. In any case, having your parent live with you instead of moving to a facility means that benefits and consequences must be considered.

The Benefits of the Multigenerational Home

- It offers more personal care to the parent.

- The entire family cares for older family members.

- It teaches children to give to others as you role model compassion.

- It is less expensive than a facility or hiring someone to give full-time care.

- The parent's recovery is enhanced with love and support.

- Familiar surroundings are comforting to the parent.

- There will be less worries about the parent falling or being alone at night.

- The parent can participate in family living, helping according to his capabilities with housework or caring for children.

A Look at the Possible Consequences

- The parent feels that she has lost some privacy and independence.

- Your family will lose some privacy and independence.

- Your parent may feel that he is a burden to you.

- You may feel overwhelmed by the increased work load.

- There may be an added expense to the family's budget.

- The extra person could cause conflict in the family.

- Children may feel resentment if they have to curtail evening activities.

- If the parent is ill, the twenty-four-hour care giving could become difficult.

FACING THE ISSUES

The new issues you will face when the parent moves into the multigenerational home are many, but the following two are most common.

The Issue of Communication. The need to communicate openly is very important. When Tom's eighty-eight-year-old mother moved into his home, the tension was obvious. "It was a move that I made without really consulting my wife or kids," Tom admitted. "I went to Mom's one day after hearing of some burglaries in her neighborhood, packed up her bags, and brought her home.

"For the next two weeks, no one spoke to me. Mom was mad because I 'bulldozed' her into moving. My wife was angry because she had not been consulted, and the kids had to share a room and give theirs to Grandma. It was a no-win situation."

Tom finally resolved the problem with a family meeting and open communication. "One night after work I asked my kids and wife to meet me at a local restaurant. After dinner, we aired grievances and talked about how to make this work. By the end of the meal, everyone was laughing and deciding that this was the best way to meet Grandma's needs. We went home and had a meeting that included Grandma and let her air her feelings. I realized that it had to be a joint decision in order for our new extended family to stay united."

The Issue of Control. Control is another issue of great concern to the parent and adult child. Your parent is as used to having control of the home as you are. You will fear losing your authority as your parent moves in, and your parent may fear becoming dominated. Careful planning and communication can make the best of these situations. Being aware of common problems that may arise and addressing them beforehand is vital.

AN ADDED BENEFIT

Studies show that children who have strong ties to older people, such as grandparents who live with them, are more emotionally secure, realize that their family is strong, and and have fewer concerns about aging. Grandparents can enable youth to have wisdom from their years of experience, and young people can give enthusiasm to the elderly.

MOVING DAY

You have done your homework, and with your parent's involvement, the decision is made to move Mom or Dad into your home. It is important now to hold another family meeting, this time including your spouse (if married), your children, and your parent as you discuss the new "rules of respect and love" for each other.

- Discuss how important open communication is between you, your spouse, your children, and your parent. If anyone has not openly discussed feelings regarding the move, now is the time to do so if it can be positive and does not hurt members.

- Plan a scheduled meal and family meeting once a week (or twice a month, if that suits your family best). Tell members that anyone can call a family meeting sooner if a problem arises that cannot wait to be resolved. This gives everyone a voice in decision making and can defuse potential problems before feelings are hurt or someone gets angry.

- Talk about finances and how expenses will be shared (you may want to do this without the children present, if it is a private matter). What is your parent expected to pay for? When should this money be given to you? What are you paying for?

If a bedroom, bath, or private outside entry must be added, will the parent help to pay for this? Be clear so there are no misunderstandings in the months ahead.

- Discuss the right for privacy that each member has and how to make sure everyone respects each other's need. Consider making a separate entrance to your parent's room and installing a private bathroom, if affordable and wanted. Privacy is especially important to children and teens. They may not express this need, but they will feel tension if they have no alone time.

- Discuss discipline with the children. They do not need three or four adults telling them what to do. Try to continue the parent/child and grandparent/child relationships. Remain the primary disciplinarian, unless the child is doing something that is dangerous or the parent is not at home. It may be difficult for the grandparent to refrain from taking over the job of "parent," but it is important for your child's well-being.

- Discuss various family members' schedules. Decide where to put a family calendar so everyone can write appointments, duties, dates, meetings, or anything else that would affect the family. Have members check the calendar each morning to make sure no conflicts occur.

- Besides a family calendar, place a notebook by each telephone. Date the top of each page. Ask each family member to write down the name of any callers and any message. You can have members tape any messages on a central bulletin board.

- Talk about compromise. Remind all family members that everyone must give in some way, and compromise is the only way to make this work.

- Do not major on the minors, especially at first. If a problem arises that causes conflict, deal with this quickly before it explodes. Be kind but firm about family rules and expectations.

- Encourage your parent to join you and your family in worship and family devotions. This could draw the unit together and open lines of communication as you lean on the *agape* (selfless) love that Christ taught. Going to worship services together is also important.

- Give your parent a job according to her ability. This may include being in charge of answering the phone during the morning hours, reading stories to children at night, tearing coupons out of magazines, or sweeping the kitchen each morning. If she can feel important to the family, her attitude and involvement will be positive.

COPING WITH LOSS

The reality is that you very likely will move your parent, whether to your home or to another facility. Understanding the sense of loss your parent feels will help make this transition smoother. Give your parent as much time as possible to adjust to the new decision. Remember, she will be leaving friends and neighbors, a home full of memories, and perhaps a pet.

As your parent deals with the loss of his home and says good-bye to that part of his life, he should bring those personal items that continue the memories of home. The section on nursing homes later in this chapter gives some ideas on items to consider.

If you can afford it, hire someone to help you when your parent first moves in. You could hire a housekeeper once or twice a week to allow you quality time with your parent. Or you could hire a caregiver for your parent for two mornings to give you quiet time or time to visit friends. Review the possible outside assistance available in chapter 4. Call your Area Agency on Aging and find out which services your parent qualifies for and apply for those that will help.

PROTECT YOURSELF

When your parent moves in with you and your family, the chances are great that you will face burnout. We discussed this thoroughly in chapter 1, but now that your parent lives with you, the stress will seem overbearing at times.

What can you do? The suggestions are many:

- Keep balance. Weigh the responsibility you have toward your family with the need to care for your parent.

- Pace yourself. Do not take on more than you can handle at home or work. Knowing this ahead of time will enable you to avoid doing too much and feeling sorry for it later.

- Get priorities in order. Drop those time-zappers that can wait or really are not necessary at this time.

- Drop unnecessary responsibilities. You need to use that time to stabilize your family. If your volunteer work is really a source of strength to you, put it on your list of priorities and drop something else to make room for the change in your schedule.

- Use family leave. Check with your employer to see if the Family Leave Bill would allow you to take time off from work while you settle your parent into the new situation.

- Let friends help. The demands of caring for an additional family member will become overwhelming if you do not delegate responsibilities.

- Meet with your pastor. If you feel the load is too heavy, your pastor can give a listening ear.

- Divide the family work up. Give more responsibilities to your children and your spouse.

- Use your city's Area Agency on Aging. Get ideas on resources that are available for your parent.

- Get a home health evaluation for your parent. Ask her physician as this will probably be covered under Medicare and may give you more ideas for assistance.

- Rethink your day. Look at the number of trips and carpools you make and the way you run your errands. Keep an index card by your keys, and write your plans for each day.

- Continue to be "good enough." Remember that no one can be perfect! Be as organized as you can be, and try innovative ways to coordinate your daily schedule.

Balance, communication and *compassion* for the needs of others are all keys to successful caregiving in the multigenerational family setting. Being human will keep you from being perfect, so relax and enjoy these years with your family.

CONGREGATE HOUSING/BOARD AND CARE HOMES

Congregate housing and board and care are popular alternatives to home care. These give your parent the feeling of being in her own apartment while being near peers that share similar situations in life. This long-term care facility is an alternative to living alone at home or moving to a nursing home. Many seniors—married and widowed—choose congregate housing as it offers a degree of independence with support services on site. The apartment-like complex offers at least one daily shared meal in a common room to encourage sociability.

Some support services may be offered in the congregate housing complex, including light housekeeping, personal care, medical care, transportation, and moderate supervision. Some complexes offer prearranged activities from field trips to craft classes to recreational activities such as bridge, bingo, or outdoor sports.

CHECK IT OUT

Some important features to check before signing a contract include:

Total Cost. Get in writing the total cost, including any extra charges for items such as laundry or activities fees. Also get in writing any rate increases that may occur within the upcoming years.

Rules and Regulations. Get in writing all rights and rules for the residents.

Grievance Procedure. Understand what the exact method is at this complex.

Residential Opinions. Talk to residents and ask questions to see if the complex is truly as described.

Security. Check out the security measures to see if it is up to standards. Is there twenty-four-hour security with entry by key only? Does the room have an electronic medical alert system? Are smoke alarms and sprinklers installed in each room?

Meal Plan. Ask about the meal plan. Does your parent have a choice of foods? Can the plan meet special dietary requirements? Are the meals well-balanced? Are they selected by a registered dietitian?

Furnishings and Cleanliness. Thoroughly check the apartment your parent will live in for cleanliness and safety. Will it be furnished or unfurnished? Will it be repainted before moving date?

Will carpets be cleaned or replaced and appliances checked? Are separate apartments reserved for a nonsmoker or smoker?

Utilities. Are the utilities included in the contract rate? What is the monthly estimate for utilities?

Noise Level. Is the apartment quiet enough for your parent?

Recreational Activities. Do the social activities appeal to your parent? Do the residents have a say in what type of activities are available? Can they choose their own level of involvement?

Transportation. What type of transportation is available for shopping, doctors' appointments, or religious services? Do residents pay extra for this service?

Medical Care. Is there a qualified doctor, nurse practitioner, or registered nurse on staff twenty-four hours a day? How close is the nearest hospital? Will the resident's health be monitored, such as blood sugar levels checked if diabetic?

Cancellation Policy. If your parent gets sick, what is the policy if your parent must move to a medical facility? Be sure to get any cancellation stipulations in the contract.

Congregate housing may be ideal for the parent who still wants privacy but needs an available social outlet. These residences usually cost less than a nursing home and are becoming very popular throughout the nation.

Group Residence

The group residence accommodation may be an apartment or home that provides several people with a bedroom, single or shared bath, and a common living area. These facilities may be publicly or privately shared. Some require that the resident participate in the care of the home by helping in the daily chores. Group residence provides a protected environment with some independence and appeals to many seniors that like companionship.

Retirement Community

A retirement community could meet many needs for those who do not want to live at home but need independence, safety, and support services. These facilities offer various levels of care, including independent living, assisted care, and nursing home care. Some retirement communities offer home health care to residents who reside in independent apartments, allowing them to stay at their "home" after major surgery or illness. Some continuing care retirement communities offer subacute nursing care for the frail elderly or the seriously ill, keeping them from hospitalization or nursing home stays. These facilities provide nutritious meals, including special dietary needs, round-the-clock security, and a well-planned social schedule.

Retirement communities usually have a staff chaplain or access to local churches, and many have gift shops, a variety of classes to fill the day, a bank, post office, beauty salons, health clinic, and a library. Within the community, residents have access to physical therapists, occupational therapists, speech therapists, and other specialists.

WHO WOULD BENEFIT?

This type of facility is for the fairly independent senior adult and can be a relief from the daily care and maintenance of a home and lawn. The daily programs encourage important mental and physical activity and allow your parent to reactivate his social life. With classes such as pottery, golf, water aerobics, creative writing, computers, and woodworking, your parent can remain vital and stay mentally sharp.

UNDERSTANDING THE COSTS

Retirement communities can have a waiting list fee, an entry fee, and a monthly fee for services or they can charge one set monthly fee. These costs vary according to the benefits offered and type of housing provided. Again, be certain to get all costs in writing.

CHECK IT OUT

Medical Care. Check with your parent's physician and find out if medical needs would be met at this facility. Again, be certain that twenty-four-hour medical care is offered and that a medical facility is close by.

Fees. Get all costs, including projected increases in writing. Have this reviewed by an attorney.

Daily Services. Get all support services offered at the retirement community in writing, including housekeeping, security, meals, health care, transportation, social activities, laundry, or any other services you feel are important.

Residents' Association. Do the residents have an association or legal way to make their wishes and concerns known?

Religious Needs. Ask how religious needs are met. Is there a chaplain on staff? Does the facility provide transportation to religious services?

Emergencies. What would happen if your parent became ill and had to go to a medical care facility? Would the contract be terminated if he could not return? What is the family's responsibility financially?

Residents' Opinions. Spend time at the facility and talk to residents and family members.

Special Illnesses. Is the staff trained to handle early stage problems with Alzheimer's patients?

Visitation Policies. Are there special visiting hours?

Grievance Policy. If your parent has a problem with the facility, what is the grievance policy?

Bill of Rights. What are the clients' rights at the complex?

Security. Is there twenty-four-hour security with entry by key only? Does the apartment or room have an electronic medical alert system with access in the bedrooms, bathrooms, and living area? Are smoke alarms and sprinklers installed in each room?

The retirement community offers the active senior a secure place to live while he is in reasonably good health. It caters to seniors who do not need constant and continual care and allows them to maintain self-esteem and personal health while relieving them from the duties of owning a home.

ECHO HOUSING

ECHO (Elder Cottage Housing Opportunity) is a small self-contained home placed in the back or side yard of a single-family home. This is an excellent consideration for adult children who want their parent nearby while providing the senior adult with independence and privacy.

These homes are economical for most families, and a five-hundred-square-foot unit usually costs under $25,000. The standard model has two bedrooms and can be built in the same style as the home it is placed next to.

The Area Agency on Aging in your community and local zoning board can give you more information on obtaining this type of alternate housing for a parent. Each community has varying restrictions on zoning, utility connections, and the architectural design required. If you live in a suburban neighborhood, you may find that such structures are prohibited by your area homeowners' association. Be sure to ask questions before you invest in this.

WHEN TO CHOOSE A NURSING HOME

Nursing homes meet the need for aging adults who must have supervision and medical care twenty-four hours a day. Recent studies show that Americans over the age of sixty-five have a 50 percent chance of entering a nursing home. Of those, one half will stay for an average of two and a half years.[1]

Nursing homes offer varying levels of supervision and medical care. *Skilled nursing care* includes twenty-four-hour supervision by a registered nurse in coordination with your parent's physician. Facilities that offer *intermediate care* provide nursing care for patients, but less medical care is needed as the patient can still take care of most personal needs. *Custodial care* is the most common type and is for patients who need help with eating, taking medications, bathing, dressing, and more.

MEETING THE STANDARDS

Nursing homes have to meet certain criteria for certification. Be certain to discuss this with the administrator of the nursing home. He will provide you, upon request, with the results of the facility's last certification.

Nursing homes should provide residents with certain basic rights, including the right to privacy and a safe and decent living environment, free from abuse and neglect; to be treated with consideration, dignity, and individuality; privacy; to use his or her own clothes and other personal property in his or her immediate living quarters, except when the facility can demonstrate that it would be unsafe, impractical, or an infringement upon the rights of other residents; to unrestricted private communication access, including receiving and sending unopened correspondence, a tele-

---

1. *New York Times*, (October 14, 1990).

phone, and visiting with any person of his or her choice at any time between the hours of 9 A.M. and 9 P.M., at a minimum. [2]

UNDERSTANDING THE COSTS

One woman had enjoyed a comfortable retirement until her husband went into the nursing home. "Since that date," she said, "we have lived in poverty."

The high costs of nursing homes can rob seniors of any hope of retirement. Studies show that approximately one fourth of those residents in nursing homes will live there for more than one year, while one in ten will remain more than three years. The average cost of one year in a nursing home in the United States is $30,000 but can exceed $80,000, depending on the care required. Medicare pays for very limited long-term care in a nursing home. It will pay for up to one hundred days of skilled care in a nursing home after discharge from a hospital when the patient stayed at least three days. Sometimes it will only cover skilled nursing care in the home for up to thirty-eight days. After that, the bills are picked up either by the individual or Medicaid. Medicare will not pay for a stay in a nursing home if the only services received are personal care. Some reports reveal that 70 percent of all single people who are admitted to nursing homes go broke within three months.

Medicaid will pay nursing home costs but usually only after the patient has depleted all personal financial assets and is next to poverty level—and if there is a Medicaid bed available. Most nursing homes have a limited number of Medicaid beds, and if they are full, your parent must wait until one is available. Call your local social security or Medicaid office for information.

CHECK IT OUT

Get referrals. Check with the physician on suggested nursing home options that would specifically meet your parent's needs and family's budget.

Talk to the hospital discharge team. They are there to help you make decisions about your parent's future care.

Use your network. Talk to your parent's pastor, friends, or anyone who has researched this subject.

---

2. Stephen G. Prom, Esq., "Nursing Home Residents' Bill of Rights," *Living Well Today* (September 1994), 9.

Spend time at the nursing home. Visit the home at different times of day and observe the residents. Do they seem happy and cared for? Is there an active residents' council and volunteer program? Does it smell clean? Do staff members treat patients with compassion and dignity?

Talk to the families and residents. Are there lounge areas to visit with friends and family? Are there activity rooms where the residents can enjoy games and fellowship?

Get everything in writing. Make sure services needed, such as physical or occupational therapy, are listed. Do they provide housekeeping, personal care, laundry, transportation, access to religious services, and companionship for no extra fee?

Review special needs. Is there a special wing for Alzheimer's patients? Are the staff members trained in the proper care of this type of patient? What about special nutritional needs?

Check the license. Does the facility have a current operating license? Does the administration have a current up-to-date state license? Is the facility a certified Medicare provider?

Look for safety features. Does the facility provide safety features that prevent accidents? Does it comply with the state or federal fire and safety codes? Does it meet disability standards with ramps, wide hallways, and grab bars?

See the patient's bill of rights. All facilities have this on file for every patient, and it is important to have a copy of this in case these rights are violated.

Consider sudden illness. What if your parent is in the intermediate facility and gets sick? What if he goes to the hospital? What if he cannot return to the intermediate facility and needs skilled care? Make certain the facility has a policy for transition to skilled care if needed by patient. If your parent only needs the skilled facility for a short period, can he move back to the intermediate facility?

Ask about personal response and assistance. Is a physician on call for emergencies? How long does it take a resident to get a response from the nursing home staff when he calls? Are patients assisted with eating or other personal care when needed?

Check with your attorney. Have an attorney that is familiar with legal affairs of the elderly carefully check contracts and rights of patients before signing. Be sure that it is clear who is paying the bill. If your parent runs out of money, are you responsible or could he apply for Medicaid?

Talk with your parent. Make sure your parent is a part of the decision-making process. Moving to a nursing home is a major change for your parent and needs to be done in a way that does not rob him of his independence. The discharge nurse can advise you on the best way to let your parent participate.

Prepare for the move. When the decision is made and the contract is signed, prepare for the move. Check with the home to see what the patient is allowed to bring. Let your parent make a list and do the best you can to accommodate the special items that will make the move easier. The room will feel much more like home if your parent can bring that special chair, heirlooms, pictures of the family, wall hangings or paintings, books, and hobbies.

Seek personal counseling. Speak with your parent's physician, the nurse at the nursing home, pastor, or anyone that can guide you on how to best help your parent deal with the change. Realize that it will take time to adjust.

Keep Your Parent's Dignity

The granddaughter of eighty-five-year-old Jonathan, a retired railroad CEO, told this story:

> I was visiting Pop a few months ago, and I brought some photographs of us when I was a child and set them on his night stand. One photograph was of us standing by a shiny engine; the other was of Pop holding me as a baby. When the nurse's aid came to bring his lunch, I asked her what she thought about Pop. She was weary and said she saw just another depressed elderly man. When his doctor came in later that afternoon, I asked him the same question. He seemed so academic and told me that he saw a eighty-five-year-old male with heart disease and depression. I looked at Pop, then at the pictures of us thirty years ago, and told the doctor that I saw a vibrant man with twinkling eyes who ran a large company and used to hold me on his knees and tell me I was his princess. At that moment Pop squeezed my hand as if to say, "Thank you." When his doctor left, Pop looked at me and said, "I'm so glad you see me as a vibrant grandfather instead of a depressed, old man. I feel like the same man I was in my youth but my body has worn out." When Pop drifted off to sleep, I took the pictures of him when he was fifty-five-years old and taped it to his door. I wanted everyone who came to care for my pop to see who he really was and treat him with dignity. My grandfather deserved that.

Sometimes in a nursing home, or any health care facility for that matter, medical workers need to be reminded that this is not just "another elderly man or woman who is filling a bed." If you find that workers are condescending to your parent, intervene and tell them of your loved one's special strengths and gifts. Let them know that you expect them to respect your parent.

FOSTER HOMES FOR ADULTS

Foster homes for adults are another possibility for your parent, although this program is not available in every community. The foster parent program is similar to the program for children, except that the family takes in a frail elderly person to live in their home. This family provides room and board and someone to be with the person. They receive money for this care from the social security office. The foster home program is available to the disabled and low income elderly, and individuals who have supplemental security income (SSI) can receive subsidies to participate in this program. To be eligible, the participant must be ambulatory and be able to carry out minimal personal functions. If your parent requires constant medical care, she may not be eligible. Contact your local social security office for more information.

CARING FOR THE ALZHEIMER'S PATIENT

Alzheimer's disease, the silent epidemic, is the fourth leading cause of death for American adults (after heart disease, cancer, and stroke), accounting for more than 150,000 deaths per year. Some studies estimate 2.5 million Americans are afflicted with Alzheimer's disease or an estimated 7 to 9 percent of those over sixty-five. Other findings report as many as four million Americans with this disease. While this disease most commonly affects those 65 and older, it strikes younger adults as well. On average, the disease lasts seven to nine years, but can go on as long as twenty years or more.

Contrary to opinion, Alzheimer's disease is not caused from a "hardening of the arteries" and is not part of the natural aging process. In no way did the patient cause the disease to occur; alcoholism does not stimulate it, and it is not related to depression.

The good news is that Alzheimer's is not communicable, while the disturbing truth is that unlike other causes of dementia, Alzheimer's has no cure.

Persons with Alzheimer's disease may show symptoms, such as forgetfulness, and they often blame these lapses on fatigue or grief. They will experience personality changes, a loss of spontaneity, and a declined interest in life's daily activities. Nighttime may bring restlessness, and hygiene and daily tasks may slip with common questions asked over and over again. Eventually the patient may be unable to speak, write, or understand what is spoken or written. The patient may become unfamiliar with those around him or unable to recognize his own image. Sometimes the patient loses his ability to feed himself, chew, or swallow. In time, the patient becomes bedridden and incontinent, and at some point, the patient may lose consciousness and will only survive with total twenty-four-hour care.[3]

THE EMOTIONS OF ALZHEIMER'S

If your parent has Alzheimer's disease, the chances are great that you are living with the confusion, anger, guilt, frustration, and grief that goes with this. Many children of Alzheimer's patients feel that they are taking care of a stranger. "Where did my mother go?" one woman cried after visiting her mother in the nursing home. "It seems like yesterday that she was a vibrant woman and leader in our community, and now she does not even know her name when I speak to her."

Because it is often difficult and expensive to get support services for these patients, the work load becomes demanding, including ongoing bathing, toileting, dressing, feeding, lifting, guarding, and basically giving up a personal life.

The only way for the caregiver to have a private life when caring for a parent with Alzheimer's is to get help as the patient's health begins to decline. At first, your friends and relatives may be able to give you some rest, but as the disease progresses you will need to hire a trained caregiver who understands the disease and knows how to watch for warning signs that the patient may become out of control.

---

3. *AARP Coping and Caring,* Revised 1991.

SEEK INFORMATION

If your city has a chapter of ADRDA (Alzheimer's Disease and Related Disorders Association), call to see what the latest information is on the disease and what is available in your community for services and financial aid. One select resource is *The 36 Hour Day*, by Nancy L. Mace and Peter V. Rabins, M.D. This caregiver's manual addresses the daily problems that you may face while caring for your parent.

As you seek information, ask if you can enroll your parent in a wanderer's program. This program assigns an identifying number to your parent and gives you a bracelet or necklace for the parent to wear. If your parent does wander off, the bracelet or necklace will have a number to identify your parent, and the organization will tell her how to get in touch with you.

WHEN TO CHOOSE ALTERNATE LIVING ARRANGEMENTS

You will have an opportunity to become informed on alternate arrangements for your parents in the early stages of the disease. This is when your research on nursing homes in your area will become invaluable. Until your parent qualifies for full-time care, check on adult day cares that provide medical attention as some do take Alzheimer's patients. Describe your parent's symptoms and behavior carefully; some facilities do not take patients that are incontinent or combative.

THE COST OF CARE

Alzheimer's disease is now considered to be our nation's third most expensive disease after heart disease and cancer. Recent reports estimate that it costs more than $210,000 to care for an Alzheimer's patient for the usual four years between diagnosis and death, with two thirds of these costs considered indirect, or not covered by any insurance plan. This staggering six-figure cost is on top of other medical expenses. Round-the-clock care in a nursing home can cost about $40,000 a year, and for those patients who stay at home, the cost is estimated at about $20,000 per year, not including the cost of loss of work for the caregiver. By the year 2030, our country's bill for Alzheimer's patients is expected to be more than $750 billion.

It is a catch-22 to receive financial aid for the person with Alzheimer's. At this time, to receive Medicare payment for the patient, he must enter the hospital for any problem other than Alzheimer's disease (diabetes, a heart condition, pulmonary problems, etc.), and then go to a nursing home for the other health problem. The patient who is admitted must require skilled nursing care and be a candidate for physical therapy. Medicaid coverage will differ, depending on which state you live in. Check with your local social security office to see if your parent will qualify. Also read your parent's private insurance policy to see if there is any coverage for Alzheimer's disease.

Understanding Hospice Care

Hospice is home care for the terminally ill. A 1992 Gallup Poll revealed that if faced with a terminal illness, nine out of ten Americans would prefer to be cared for in either their own home or a family member's home.

With more than two thousand hospice programs throughout the country, the chances are great that one is within your range. Hospice care is for anyone with a life-limiting illness for which medical treatment or cure is no longer possible or desired, and cancer patients comprise the majority of these patients. Hospice focuses on the terminally ill patients and their families by providing special services, including nursing, psychological, social, spiritual care, and volunteer assistance while working with your physician. Many hospices accept patients who have no live-in caregiver or whose caregiver is disabled, and some hospices provide a wide range of service to terminally ill patients in nursing homes.

The hospice staff and trained volunteers offer bereavement support to families following the death of the loved one. Hospice provides the most effective care while minimizing the use of unwanted treatment.

Medicare covers hospice care as do some private insurance companies, HMO's, and Medicaid programs. Charitable support to hospice covers those that have no coverage. A recent study for the Health Care Finance Administration found that Medicare saved about $1.26 for every $1.00 spent on hospice. Traditional home care services were found to be about 30 percent more expensive than hospice care during the last twenty-four weeks of life.

While your referring physician can continue working on your treatment plan, you can also call your local hospice. For information, contact the National Hospice Organization, 1901 N. Moore St., Suite 901, Arlington, VA 22009 (703-243-5900).

MAKING THE RIGHT CHOICE

When deciding on a long-term care facility, you need to decide which facility or situation will best meet your parent's need, including affordability. Check through the options listed in this chapter and weigh the advantages and disadvantages. Also check on the criteria to qualify for Medicaid in chapter 10. Review the facts, talk with your parent and family members, and then make the best decision you can together.

6

SAFEGUARDING YOUR PARENT'S HOME

How many of us consider safety features when we purchase a new home? Most of us consider the location, the style or roominess, the layout and design, the desired amenities such as large closets and kitchen, tile or hardwood floors, or even a screened lanai with pool. But with more than 70 percent of the population suffering from a disability at least once during their lifetime, perhaps we need to rethink the home situation and make safety the top priority. Especially with our aging population, home and outdoor environments must be reworked to handle the mobility and vision problems of the elderly or disabled.

This chapter will focus on prevention as we discuss simple, inexpensive changes you can make to safeguard your parent's home. Whether from a weakness in ankles, knees, or hips, the chances of falling at home increase greatly with age. These falls are caused by physical problems ranging from unsteadiness, thinning bones, or weakness in muscles, to dizziness, heart problems, and medications that can disorient the person.

Other problems that cause falls and injuries are often difficult to identify and at times are simply the result of carelessness. Tripping over objects such as furniture, telephone cords, and rugs could be avoided if considered carefully. Good lighting in an elderly person's home, especially at night, may also result in fewer falls and limit this risk factor.[1]

Studies show that each year more than one third of all people over age sixty-five fall at least once. While only 10 percent of these falls lead to serious injuries, falling can push an elderly person into self-imposed immobility, dependence, and even depression.

Whether your parent is weakened from a heart condition, visual problems, arthritis or other ailments, steps can be taken, including purchasing assistive devices, to make the living environment safer. You can check with local medical supply houses to find the latest in assistive and safety devices to install in your parent's home. One federally funded agency, Abledata (1-800-227-0216), has a data base which provides lists of adaptive devices and distributors.

Local chapters of the AARP can give information on renovation to make the home safe and livable for seniors. You might check with health agencies such as the American Arthritis Association, the American Heart Association, or the American Cancer Society to ask about specific ailments and the necessary safety devices available. Also ask your parent's doctor for suggestions on where to turn for safety information.

TAKING CONTROL

By taking control over your parent's home environment (or room in a retirement facility or nursing home), you can help him or her avoid unexpected falls or injuries. Let the following tips help you become alert to the safety measures that can be taken—before an accident occurs.

HOME ENTRY

Many accidents occur when someone first enters a home, whether from tripping on a hose or missing the step on the front porch.

---

1. Harris H. McIlwain, et al., *Winning with Osteoporosis* (New York: John Wiley and Sons, Inc., 1994), 34.

- Make sure that the sidewalk and stones are level on the entrance to the front door.

- Remind your parent to keep water hoses coiled next to the house.

- Check to make sure the doormat is flat on ground level with no flipped-up edges.

- Provide adequate lighting during day and evening hours.

- Check dead bolts on the door and make sure they are adequate.

LIVING ROOM

Although the living room is a more spacious room, problems can occur if a parent trips on a frayed rug or slippery wooden floor or if he falls trying to get up from a low, soft coach.

- Make certain that tables, chairs, and couches are the proper height (hips should never be lower than the knees) so the person does not have a fear of falling as he sits down.

- Check chairs and couches to see if they are firm and have strong arms.

- Survey the lighting and make sure no cords are in walkways.

- Window blinds that open during daytime hours and close tightly at night are easy to manipulate for the elderly and give a sense of privacy.

- Make sure entrances, foyers, doorways, and halls are free of obstructions.

- Purchase rubber lever handles for all doors if grip is a problem.

- Anchor rugs, carpeting, or doormats so they cannot be lifted. You can purchase safety strips to keep these in place.

- Replace old electrical cords or extension cords. Multiple sockets could present a possible fire hazard.

- Purchase remote control units that turn off the television, lights, and appliances without cords.

- Make certain that the fireplace is sealed with a screen or glass enclosure. Have the fireplace cleaned annually, if it is used, and make sure the chimney is open. Check for leaks in a gas fireplace.

- Be sure that electrical wiring throughout the house is sound. Have this inspected, if unsure.

STAIRWAY

According to the Consumer Product Commission (1982), in 1981 approximately one million Americans received emergency room treatment due to stair-related injuries. And, more than 854 stair-related deaths occurred among adults over age sixty-five. [2]

- Make sure stairs are well-lit and have a solid banister or railing on both sides.

- Install a smoke alarm at the top of the stairs and check regularly for operation.

- Make sure no clutter or throw rugs impedes the walkway to and up the stairs.

- Tape a neon strip to the stairs to help orient your parent, or if you choose to paint the stairs, use colors such as red and yellow. Studies show that older people need two to three times as much illumination as younger people. Falls occur most often on the top and bottom steps.

- Place a flashlight at the bottom and top of the stairs.

- Make sure the steps are of equal height and that the treads are not worn.

- Be sure your parent's pajamas and robe are not too long, and provide her with sturdy shoes to wear during evening hours.

---

2. "The Perfect Fit," *AARP*, 1992, 34.

- Put a small basket or plastic carrier off to the side of the stairs to put items in to carry up and down. This frees one arm to hold the rail when taking items up and down.

BATHROOM

Bathroom safety presents many problems as these rooms are usually the smallest rooms in the home, yet most frequently used. The frail elderly find it quite difficult to maneuver in this small space, including sitting, standing, climbing in and out of tubs, and turning around. Problems can be due to inadequate lighting, a wet floor, scalding from hot water, and more. Yet even a large bathroom is not the answer; as simple a move as reaching for soap or a towel may cause falls.

Studies show that one out of every ten elderly burn victims are injured from bathing in water that is too hot, and a check of homes of the elderly show that only about 6 percent of the homes have skid proof rugs or no rugs.)

Below are some bathroom safety tips.

- Turn the water temperature on the hot water heater down to 120 degrees or lower depending on what is safe for your parent.

- Get your parent in the habit of always checking the temperature of the tub water with her wrist before stepping into the tub.

- Install grab bars beside toilet area. While many people use the towel rack for a grab bar, this can be very dangerous when it pulls out of the wall.

- Purchase a raised toilet seat that fits on top of the regular toilet, or if your parent fears getting up in the middle of the night, get a bedside commode to use.

- Make sure there are no electrical appliances in the bathroom that could shock your parent if wet.

- Install grab bars in bathtub area and also purchase a suction-cup rubber mat. Make sure this mat runs the length of the tub and has a nonslip service.

The bathroom also needs:

- clothing hooks on back of door that are within easy reach

- cloth shower curtain instead of glass shower doors

- a nonskid stool with a back to place in the tub

- a hand-held shower head

- soap on a rope

- terry mitt for bathing

- shower caddie to hold shampoo and toiletries

- terry robe to dry off with and put on after bath

- a tub transfer bench for wheelchair bound adults

- nonskid chair in front of sink, if parent is ill or weak

KITCHEN

Accidents occur with frequency in the kitchen for the elderly. Not only do they have to contend with the dangers of hot water, electricity, gas, and knives, but many elderly people slip on wet floors, get sprayed with hot grease, and drop canned items on feet.

Although falling is the leading type of home accident, burns are a close second. According to the National Burn Information Exchange, cooking, smoking, use of matches, and bathing are the greatest burn risks.[3]

- Install a smoke alarm and check regularly.

- Purchase a special lever for the kitchen sink faucet that makes it easier for those with arthritic hands or those who are weak.

- Consider putting the shelves on casters to keep from having to reach deep into cabinet. You can also put items on a Lazy Susan or install pull-out shelves.

- Keep medications and poisons out of the reach of grandchildren. Consider a locked box for these.

---

3. Ibid.

- Install a peg board for storing pots and utensils. This should be visible and easily accessible. Make sure all pots and utensils have easy grab handles. Peg boards on the back of cabinets and doors also make items easy to reach.

- Purchase large pull handles to attach to the knobs on the cabinet, making it easier for arthritic hands.

- Purchase pick-up tongs that are around two feet in length to lift objects down from a high shelf. You can find tongs with a magnet end for picking up small metal objects.

- Have your parent use pot holders, not dish towels, to pick up pots on the stove. Dish towels and loose clothing may catch on fire as they hit the hot unit.

- Use a cart with tray to move items around the kitchen.

- Make sure the lighting is bright. Use the highest wattage the unit can handle safely.

- Be sure to let your parent know that a step stool or chair should never be used to reach items as this increases the chances for falls.

- Adjust the temperature of the hot water on the water heater so it does not scald delicate skin.

- Have a timer by the stove and oven. Your parent should set the timer when she starts cooking to remind her to turn off the stove or oven at the proper time—before a fire occurs or a pot boils over.

- Make sure there are safe electrical outlets in the kitchen.

- Install a fire extinguisher and teach your parent how to use this in case of emergency.

- Check gas stove periodically for leaks.

- Remove any electrical appliances from near the kitchen sink, and remind your parent to unplug these after use. Frequently inspect these to check for mechanical failure, frayed cords, or loose plugs.

- Store household cleaners, bleach, ammonia, bug sprays, or other substances away from food items. It is best to keep these away from counters too.

BEDROOM

Not only does the bedroom present a problem for many elderly, this room is also used at night, when vision is decreased.

- Install smoke alarms outside bedroom door and check regularly.

- Make certain that the entryway is no higher than one half inch to discourage tripping.

- Provide adequate lighting, with a closet light on during the night or nightlights in the room and hallway leading to the bathroom or stairway.

- Make sure the reading chair is firm, and add a cushion if needed.

- Clean out the drawers and closet and throw away useless items to make every item easily accessible.

- Get rid of clutter, debris, and throw rugs in the bedroom.

- Check to see if the bed covers fit tightly and do not slip. Often elderly people fall when their comforter has slipped off the bed unknowingly and tangles around their legs.

- Install a telephone next to your parent's bedside with a voice activated device, if needed. If the phone is hand-held, make sure it is light weight. Push button phones are easy for most elderly people to use.

- Put an enlarged knob on the bedside lamp so that it is easy to turn on, especially for those with weakness or arthritis. Another device enables your parent to clap his hands and the light will turn on or off.

- Purchase a hospital bed with grab bars for a railing. On a hospital bed, you can lower and raise the top and bottom to a convenient, safe level. This is especially beneficial for a weak or arthritic person as the guard rail offers extra support.

- Have a bedside commode accessible, as well as a lamp and flashlight by the bed, if your parent fears getting up in the middle of the night.

- Remind your parent to never smoke in bed, and have a smoke alarm installed in the room.

- Have the space heater checked and anchored in a safe place. Carefully monitor the temperature for your parent's needs.

- Establish an emergency medical information card for your parents. On this, put the doctors' names and phone numbers written in large print next to the bedside telephone. Also include family members' names and numbers and the emergency medical service number. Make sure your parent has an emergency information card in clear view, in case he cannot speak due to accident or illness.

On this card, provide the following:

- your parent's name, address, phone number, age, and emergency contact,

- physician's name and number,

- a list of medications your parent is taking and dosage,

- information on any allergies your parent may have,

- present and previous illnesses,

- your parent's blood type and RH factor,

- whether your parent wears contact lenses. (If left on, they could damage the cornea.)

- Other special precautions or information.

Make several copies of this card and have your parent keep one in his or her wallet or purse and give one to a neighbor and closest relative.

Millions of Americans have medical problems and dangerous allergies which responding emergency personnel should know before using treatment. Whether the person is a diabetic who depends on regular insulin shots, a cardiovascular patient who takes anticoagulants that must be counteracted by other drugs to prevent excessive bleeding in accidents, or has arthritis and depends on corticosteroid drugs, having information available will help the emergency crew assist your parent.

SAFE DRIVING

No elderly adult wants to give up driving as this offers an outlet into the world as they seek to keep independence. Even if your parent drives only to the grocery store and to church, there are some important rules to follow.

- Talk with your parent about the new rules of driving. He should not drive in adverse weather conditions—rain, wind, fog, snow, ice, or smoke.

- See if special equipment is needed on the vehicle. She will need to compensate for any hearing or visual depth perception problems with special equipment. Have these installed by the proper authorities.

- Sign your parent up for defensive driving courses. The AARP offers an excellent eight-hour driver's training entitled 55 Alive/Mature Driving Course that shows your parent how to drive defensively. The cost is small and discounts may be given for seniors.

- Make certain that your parent's car is in excellent condition. Establish a relationship with a reputable service station in the neighborhood and have your parent go in for routine checks. Ask the owner to "look out" for your parent as he checks tires, water, fluid, and other parts. Check the wiper blades and replace these at least once a year.

- Encourage minimum speeds. Your parent will need to drive slowly as she increases in age. Reaction time may not be as quick as it used to be. Talk with him about avoiding driving during the busy times of the day, if possible.

- Provide her with a jumper cable, flashlight, and portable first aid kit for trips and distress signals.

- Talk about increased crime for elderly drivers, especially women. And emphasize the importance of always keeping seatbelts fastened and doors locked while in the car.

- Purchase a special, broad-based key handle at a medical supply store for quick entry.

- Give your parent a CB radio or cellular phone for calling for help when traveling alone.

- Discourage nighttime driving!

Personal Safety

One of the greatest fears of the elderly is personal safety. Some studies state that more than two thirds of the elderly population felt certain that they would be a victim of a violent crime when they grew older. Even when locked in a safe environment, elderly people still have the fear that if someone were to break in, they could not protect themselves. Therefore, you must do all you can to burglarproof your parent's home.

More than six million burglaries occur each year, representing one every ten seconds. More than one half of these said they did not have to force their way into the home.

- Start with a neighborhood brunch. Invite several of your parent's closest neighbors over, and talk about crime and safety. Have them trade phone numbers and house keys, and encourage them to watch out for each other's property.

- Set some rules for exiting the home. If your parent is going to be away for a period of time, it is important to leave a light on and either the television or a radio playing.

- Make sure your parent activates the house alarm, if one is installed, when she leaves. Remind your parent to lock the doors when leaving the house, even if going next door to visit with a neighbor or to water the back lawn. Always have an extra house key accessible but not hidden outside the home. This should be left at a trusted neighbor's home or carried by your parent in a small pouch or pocket. If she returns to her house after being away and the door is open, she should leave immediately, go to a neighbor, and call the police.

- Install deadbolt locks on every door. Tell your parent that these are to be locked always—whether at home or not, day or night. Always have a key accessible in case of fire. If your parent has moved into a new home or apartment, make sure all locks are changed immediately.

- Purchase hand-held emergency alert systems. These are usually small in size, lightweight, and can even be attached to a key ring. Your parent must pull the ring for a distressing alarm to sound, signifying that help is needed.

- Talk about personal safety. Encourage your parent to go with someone else when shopping.

Studies have found that criminals almost always leave older people alone if there is more than one. Teach your parent how to constantly be aware of her surroundings.

The greatest concerns for attack on the elderly are at malls, ATM machines, pay phones, parking lots, and laundries. Emphasize to your parent that he should never go to any of these places unless with friends or family. Park as close to the mall as possible, and walk in and out with a crowd of people. She should check around the car before unlocking the door and keep her purse and purchases close to her body. Should someone try to take her purse, wallet, or packages, tell your parent to give in. It is better to lose a purse than a life. Many seniors carry a wallet in a hidden pocket next to their body or wear a hip pack (a wallet attached to a belt worn around the waist).

- Ask your parent to sit near the driver when riding a bus.

- Have your parent keep a garage door opener in a pocket or purse, for immediate entrance to the home upon arrival.

- Check the doors for safety. The sliding glass doors should have a thick pin that is pushed in a hole through both doors as a safety lock, and a broom handle cut to size can be placed along the bottom metal runner to keep the doors from being opened.

Wooden doors must be well-made and secure with hinges on the inside. If the exterior doors are not sturdy, you may want to reinforce the door frame, add metal plates for the dead bolt, and consider solid hardwood doors. Secure all doors that lead to the outside, including the basement or attic doors. Make sure your parent has a front-door peephole to guard from unwanted guests.

Magnified peepholes can be installed to allow a view of a broad area. Your parent should be instructed to keep the door bolted and chained, and to look through the peephole before opening.

- Check the windows for safety. Windows should be thick, locked, or covered with safety bars. Leave one window available for an emergency exit in case of fire.

- Make sure there are smoke alarms throughout the home, and check these biannually for operation. Many seniors have a dull sense of taste and smell for various reasons—smoking, aging, medications, or dental disorders. Additional smoke detectors are helpful, if your parent has a problem. These batteries should be replaced regularly as well.

- Get a dog for your parent, if he lives alone. This should not be a large, vicious dog but one who makes a lot of racket should a stranger approach. The dog will also give your parent company providing a wonderful health benefit.

- Make certain that any pet door is small enough so a person could not come through (usually five inches or smaller).

- Check the lighting. An outdoor light can deter intruders.

- Do some behind-the-scene checks to help your parent feel safer. After talking with neighbors, let your local police know your parent is alone and elderly.

- Check with your local fire station and emergency medical service, and see if they will keep a file on the elderly in the neighborhood. Treatment can speed up if these services have a file with the contact numbers and record of illnesses.

- Some residential areas have a "neighborhood watch" or security patrol. Find out if this is available. These professionals will keep watch on your parent's home twenty-four-hours a day as they patrol the neighborhood by car. They will also alert residents if prowlers have been spotted or if burglaries take place, and some even escort people to their cars when needed.

- Consider burglar bars or security shutters if your parent lives in a high crime area. Be sure he can escape in case of fire, and always get approval from the local fire department.

BASIC HOME SAFETY

DEVISE AN EMERGENCY PLAN

Whether from fire, storm, or natural disaster, your parent needs to understand the steps to follow in case of emergency, depending on his locale.

- Talk about safety if the power goes out. Make sure your parent knows to crack a window to receive ventilation.

- Have flashlights available and accessible to avoid use of candles (a proven fire hazard). Check the batteries in these periodically.

- Have a battery-operated radio by the bed so he can hear any broadcasted emergency instructions.

- Check with the Red Cross in your community for detailed information for devising an emergency plan. After receiving this, go over it carefully with your parent.

HEAT WAVES

Researchers have now found that heat rather than heat stroke is the cause of many more deaths. Excessive heat and humidity in a home place a strain on the heart and circulatory system. For an elderly person whose health is already compromised by chronic disease, this form of heat stress may be fatal.

- Leave one window unbolted for necessary ventilation. If the main room in your parent's home is not air conditioned, and if all windows and doors are bolted for safety, be sure to have either one open window (with a lock that will keep it from raising more than six inches) or a fan to circulate air blowing over a bowl of ice cubes.

- Remind your parent to drink additional fluids on hot days. They should eat lightly and avoid cooking or eating hot foods.

- Choose appropriate clothing. On the hottest days, your parent should wear light, cotton clothing, take cool showers and baths periodically, and sponge off with cool water between baths.

- Thoroughly check fans or air-conditioning system.

COLD SPELLS

Temperatures ranging from 40 to 65 degrees over a period of days with poor heat may cause hyperthermia in the frail elderly. The likeliest victims of hyperthermia are the very old, the poor, and those whose bodies do not respond normally to cold, such as those who suffer from diseases of the veins and arteries or are being treated with certain drugs.

- Do a complete safety check on all heating units as well as fans. Check the wiring to make sure it is in good condition. If you are unsure, purchase a new unit to make sure your parent is safe. Check proper temperature for your parent's condition.

- Check with your local utility company to see who could inspect your parent's electric or gas appliances or ask an electrician to make sure that all appliances are in working order. If your parent uses a wood burning stove or fireplace, check for proper ventilation and have a glass door in front of the fireplace. Make sure the chimney is clear and vents properly.

- Keep the temperature on the thermostat regulated, and put an index card next to this to remind your parent to keep it at 72 degrees (or whatever is comfortable to her).

- Tell your parent to wear a stocking cap and socks to bed at night to maintain body temperature.

- Stay in frequent touch with your parent to ensure his wellness during hot and cold spells.

EMERGENCY TELEPHONE NUMBERS

This list of emergency numbers should be written in large print and placed by the telephone. Keep this list up-to-date.

Emergency Contact	Telephone Number
Police	
Rescue or Emergency Medical Service	
Poison Control	
Hospital Emergency	
Doctor's name and number	
Dentist's name and number	
Pastor's name and number	
All night drugstore	
Closest neighbor	
Closest relative	
Other	

To this list, attach your parent's Emergency Medical Information Card.

FIRST AID KIT

Try to keep your parent's first aid kit well-stocked. The following represent some basic items used most frequently with minor household accidents. You may know of other items that your parent would need. Put these items in a shoe box or other storage bin, and make sure your parent knows where the kit is located.

- 3 by 3 inch sterile gauze dressings

- box of plastic strips in an assortment of sizes

- roll of half-inch adhesive tape

- small tube of antibiotic ointment

- calamine lotion for poison ivy

- thermometer

- ice bag

- nonaspirin pain reliever

- antihistamine for swelling in case of allergic reactions

- tweezers for taking out splinters or pieces of glass

- sterile eye pads

- hydrogen peroxide

- cotton swabs

AN OUNCE OF PREVENTION

Taking preventive measures *before* an accident happens is especially smart with aging parents. Most adult children who spend late nights waiting in hospital emergency rooms never dreamed that their parent would trip on the bedspread in the middle of the night or that she would fall and fracture a hip while getting out of the shower. But all would admit that extra precaution is most important to ensure a safe, healthy environment for their aging parent.

7

THE BENEFITS OF EXERCISE AND ACTIVITY

Fear of falling is probably one of the greatest fears of the elderly. And because of this fear being so overwhelming, many elderly adults would rather not move at all than risk having an accident. One eighty-four-year-old gentleman, Edward, gave up his independence because he was afraid he might fall. "I lived alone and was doing fine until a few months ago," he told us. "I got up in the middle of the night and tripped on the bathroom rug. Luckily I caught myself before I hit the floor, but ever since that night, I can hardly walk from room to room without panic."

Edward told this story from his new bed at a nursing home after deciding to leave his residence of forty-nine years. Edward did not have to move to a nursing home. His physician told him that he was a healthy man, had no weakness in his legs, and could care for himself . . . but Edward allowed fear to overcome him.

Giving up independence does not have to happen to your parent, if he is actively involved in a regular program of exercise to maintain independence and mobility. When your parent has con-

trol over his body, he will have a continued sense of well-being and
feel as if he can manage most other areas of his life.

Exercise as a Part of a Healthy Lifestyle

To allow your parent to choose a sedentary life is to give up on
his or her ability to function in an active, vital, and independent
way. Inactivity feeds into the myth that with old age comes automatic decline—physical, mental, and social—and that myth certainly is not true!

Contrary to what we may believe, the thought process shows little or no decline with aging. Many studies show that disease rather
than the normal aging process reduces mental capacity. Men and
women who are physically active in middle age are more likely to
age successfully than those who are not active at all. *A landmark,
fifteen year longitudinal study of older people showed no measurable decline in many body functions until after age seventy, and very little decline
by eighty-one.* Cognitive abilities were intact to at least age seventy-
five and still intact in almost all who had reached eighty-one, although speed at rote memory declined.[1]

If your parent is healthy, he should not fall back in an easy chair
upon retirement and manipulate a channel changer for the next
twenty-five years. Studies show that once a senior adult becomes
sedentary, health and emotional problems begin to skyrocket and
can seem never ending.

Exercise Is Healing

We know that exercise helps many diseases, lowers blood pressure, lowers cholesterol, encourages bone growth, strengthens
muscles to support the body, relieves pain, reduces stress, and
more. What are the alternatives? Instead of only the normal aging
process causing physical, mental and social decline, perhaps lack
of exercise is a culprit. Now that is exciting news! Because, while
we cannot stop the aging process, we do have control of how active
we are.

---

1. Jere Daniel, "Learning to Love Growing Old," *Psychology Today* (September/
October 1994), 66.

Research with adults over age sixty show that exercise has a protective effect for both coronary state and total mortality until at least eighty years old.

For many diseases, exercise is a prescription for treatment that the patient can do at no monetary cost! Many seniors with ailments such as back pain, heart attack, osteoporosis, fractured hip and hip replacement, stroke, arthritis, and chronic pain from various diseases might benefit from added mobility and exercise.

Be sure to ask your parent's physician for careful guidance in the proper exercise plan for his or her needs and abilities.

Exercise can be done in almost any situation, whether your parent is ambulatory, in a wheelchair, or bedridden. Improved mobility, outlook, and general well-being make this an important issue for you and your parent to address.

Your parent may say, "I never exercised before. Why should I start now?" Or, "I can barely get out of bed. Don't ask me to move around more." But you should ignore your parent's argument, and listen to the experts: If aging adults become sedentary, they will rapidly decline, physically and mentally.

HOW MUCH EXERCISE IS ENOUGH?

It does not take much to make a difference in your parent's mobility. In fact, your parent only needs to exercise a minimum of twenty to thirty minutes three or four times per week and maintain an active schedule in between to really affect his quality of life. As the exercise routine becomes regular, your parent will restore lung capacity, increase endurance and strength, and feel uplifted in spirit. Not bad for merely expending a little energy!

There are many benefits of exercise and activity for the elderly. Some are as follows:

- greater mobility

- increased independence

- more control over the body

- greater range of motion

- more flexible joints

- improved muscle tone

- may ease depression

- increases circulation of blood

- aids in digestion

- aids in ending constipation

- greater social contacts

- gives mental stimulation

- controls stress

While exercise alone may not change the length of your parent's life, the quality of life can improve with an active lifestyle. Most physicians will agree that patients who lead an active and healthy life not only feel better but need to see the doctor less often.

Keys to a Healthy Life

Exercise tops the list as a main key to a healthy life. The other ingredients include:

- exercise

- healthy diet

- quit smoking

- control weight

- moderate alcohol

- adequate sleep

My Mom's Too Old

Wait, you may say, this information is great for that robust, healthy sixty-five year old who may just need some motivation, but my parent is a frail eighty-four-year-old, and she depends on me for every need. What can she do?

Keep reading. We feel that even the bedridden patient can remain active to the extent her physician approves, and this chapter will show you ways to motivate your parent to become an active family member. Your parent will participate in daily family activities and become a vital member of the daily routine. Initially, it's going to take some work, but as he becomes more active, he will profit from a new sense of self-respect, begin to feel useful, and regain a much-desired control over life again.

One study tested a group of one hundred frail nursing home patients over a ten-week period. Those who received exercise training increased muscle strength and gait velocity. The patients not receiving exercise training remained about the same or declined. Of those exercising, stair climbing ability improved. The conclusion was that in the frail elderly, high intensity resistance training exercise is a feasible and effective means of counteracting muscle weakness and physical frailty.

There are many causes of frailty such as chronic disease, sedentary lifestyle, nutritional problems, or aging itself, but these problems are potentially preventable or reversible.[2] The fear of falling, weight-bearing pain due to arthritis, and difficulty transferring from a seated to an upright position due to muscle weakness all likely lead to self-imposed restriction and immobility among the very old.

LEARN FROM CASE STUDIES

Sid visited his physician for a complete physical just before retirement. His physician said, "Sid, you are very healthy except for a little arthritis and high blood pressure. We can manage both with medication and exercise. All you need is to find a creative outlet, volunteer to help someone, and get moving. If you stay active, you'll live a long, healthy life."

Sid only heard the doctor say he had arthritis and high blood pressure, and he went into a panic. "I've been healthy my entire life," he cried to his only son. "Now it's all over. I'm a sick, old man." At age sixty-two, Sid virtually gave up, became depressed, and sat down in his recliner waiting to die, speaking of nothing but his high blood pressure and the pain of arthritis. Sid remained depressed and moody for an amazing thirty-five years. He became stiff and immobile from lack of exercise and did not really care if anyone came over to visit. He gained weight from the lack of exercise and rarely even spoke to his son because he "was so ill."

2. *The New England Journal of Medicine*, vol. 330, no. 25, (June 1994), 1769.

Sid spent more than one third of his life waiting to die when he could have filled these precious years with activity, friends, and family. Sid should have been enjoying his son and his grandchildren; but instead, his family gave up on Sid because he was so pitiful that they assumed he was going to die soon, as he said. While his wife and son catered to him, waiting on him hand and foot, they never again enjoyed being with him.

What If . . .

You have to wonder what if his son had challenged Sid at sixty-two years to take part in life? What if he had encouraged him to do something new every day and to call or write to him about it? What if Sid and his wife had taken responsibility for their physical and mental health by exercising thirty minutes three or four times each week? What if Sid had made an effort to go fishing with his grandchildren or go visit his sister at the beach instead of dwelling on minor ailments? The sad truth is that not only did Sid miss one third of his life, so did his child and grandchildren. Sid had so much to share, but instead he lost all respect for himself and felt useless and invaluable. What a loss!

Ethel's Challenge to Wellness

Ethel never left her house either until her granddaughter challenged her to wellness. She was seventy years old and had arthritis and had been given exercises by her physician to build strength. But because she had lost so much strength in her hands, she did not feel that anything would help, so she ignored the exercises.

Ethel's granddaughter, Kate, a second year nursing student, came home at Christmas break and saw the decline in her grandmother's condition. Kate had learned enough about the benefits of exercise on joint diseases in some of her courses that she knew it was worth a try.

"Grandmomma Ethel, I want you to try those exercises for arthritis for three months," Kate said. "If you do them daily, when I come home this spring, we will go to the fanciest restaurant in town for dinner."

Ethel laughed at Kate's naivety, but took the challenge "just to humor her." Guess what? The exercises worked (just as her physician had told her!), and her strength and mobility improved dramatically. Within three months, Ethel was even able to play the piano for her Sunday School class again. She went for that special dinner out and enjoyed her granddaughter's company. But even better, Ethel's confidence and self-esteem flourished; she got out more and exercised for strength and easing pain. Ethel regained control of her life. The effort was worth it to her and her family.

DISPEL THE MISCONCEPTIONS

When is exercise not helpful? How much is enough? How much is too much? What if they get injured?

Look at the following myths about exercise and understand what is really truth and what is not.

Myth: Exercise does not affect the aging process.

Truth: You do have some control over aging. You cannot affect your genetic pool or the onset of illnesses or accidents, but lack of exercise can lead to deterioration of the body and the mind. Study after study shows that exercise for seniors may affect physical as well as psychological well-being.

Myth: My parent requires bedrest because he is so weak. His physician does not understand and keeps telling him to get up, and he will feel better.

Truth: Bedrest is seldom recommended for an illness unless it is in a final stage or if it is physically impossible to move.

Always check with your parent's physician to see if bedrest is needed. Have the physician explain the consequences of total bedrest to your parent.

Myth: My parent is too depressed to exercise.

Truth: Exercise and activity can help depression. Encourage your parent to start on a program approved by his physician to help alleviate the symptoms of depression. He will start feeling better after he stays on the program for several weeks.

Myth: Weight training is for the young and athletic, not for elderly adults, especially those who have trouble walking.

Truth: Studies now show that light weight training is helpful for the elderly, if a doctor allows this. By participating in a weight training program approved by his physician, your parent can increase muscle mass. Weight training increases strength, helps mobility, and boosts a sense of well-being. In many cases, exercise enables the person to walk without assistance.

Myth: My parent is too old to begin an exercise program.

Truth: You are never too old to start an exercise program if your physician approves. Physical activity can include everything from running, biking, stationary biking, walking on a treadmill, walking out-of-doors, and weight training to gardening, mopping, sweeping, mowing the lawn, folding laundry, cooking dinner, vacuuming, and other chores.

Myth: My parent has worked his whole life and feels that we should now take care of him. He claims that he is tired, and it is his turn to rest.

Truth: Does he mean that it is his turn to rest and to deteriorate? When you start taking away the motivation to get up and do for yourself, you are taking away your parent's independence, control, and self-esteem. Even a bedridden parent or one in a wheelchair should still be participating in some way in the activities in the home until it is absolutely no longer possible.

Myth: My parent has a chronic illness, so he shouldn't exercise or participate in activities.

Truth: Studies show that almost 85 percent of older adults suffer from at least one chronic degenerative disease. These diseases challenge health care resources and diminish personal independence and vitality. Regular physical exercise and proper nutrition, maydelay the clinical symptoms of many of these diseases.

Some common reasons the elderly think they no longer need to exercise include the onset of a disease that causes decline, inability to walk, needed bedrest, various medications, changes of psychological state, changes in social state. These are problems, but they do not excuse your parent from exercise. It is time to find out what the physician recommends and to start a program that fits the problem.

Myth: My parent has never exercised. It is too late now.

Truth: It is only too late if he refuses to try to help himself. There has to be some form of exercise that would be fun and worth the challenge to your parent. Be creative and try to motivate him. Could he walk the dog around the block? Maybe she could start a garden in the backyard. What about joining several friends for a stretching class at church. Ask your parent, "What do you have to lose?" If he chooses a sedentary life, he could lose a great deal—his health, mobility, and strength. He could be faced with premature aging, much pain, and the onset of diseases that he could work toward preventing.

Myth: My parent has foot problems and can't exercise.

Truth: Some researchers report that up to 75 percent of people older than sixty-five have at least one foot problem requiring medical attention. Neglect of foot problems can cause trouble when it comes to exercising, but with proper foot care most problems can be alleviated or helped to a point that participation in some exercise can be tolerated. Ask your parent's physician for a referral to a podiatrist (foot specialist) who can solve the problem.

Myth: Light, sporadic exercise is as good as a regularly scheduled program of exercise.

Truth: Exercise needs to be a regularly scheduled plan to get the best results. This means at least four times a week or every other day, if possible. Check with your parent and his doctor to see what type of routine would best meet his needs.

GETTING STARTED

EXERCISE AS A STRESS-BUSTER

Aging causes new types of stress for the elderly as we will discuss in chapter 9. Most seniors are faced with the loss of independence and control, financial insecurity, loss of loved ones, inability to do the tasks that need to be done, fear of leaving their home, increased illness, physical decline, and isolation. All these factors cause stress.

But the good news is that exercise is a proven stress-buster, helping us cope with our everyday challenges. We may not have control over the occurrences in our life, but we do have control over the way we handle the stress produced by daily events. The tension felt each day can be disbursed through exercise rather than aimed at those around us.

Exercise can certainly help alleviate the amount of anxiety your parent suffers. By exercising twenty to thirty minutes three to four times per week, your parent will notice a reduction in heart rate, blood pressure, and cholesterol, as well as lessened anxiety.

Just a simple program including daily living tasks, sweeping, gardening, and doing chores around the home can all help relieve stress and make your parent feel like a participating member of the human race.

Exercise is the act of bodily and mental exertion. It is any stimulation that causes a reaction. This is wonderful for your parent even if it starts at a very low level of activity. Remember, some movement is better than none at all.

How to Begin

Following are tips that will give you confidence as you encourage aging parents to participate in exercise and activity:

Get medical approval. Before your parent begins any exercise or activity program always check with his physician for a complete physical. Be sure the physician approves of the program before your parent starts.

Make the challenge. Be willing to challenge your parent to do something she is not used to doing and may not want to try. You can do this creatively or be silly and dramatic, whatever it takes to get her attention. You might let that family member she has trouble saying no to make the challenge to get active.

Show determination. Be determined that this is not only good for your parent but for the entire family. While you cannot make someone do something he has an aversion to, you certainly can make your feelings known, and tell him how important activity is to his health and longevity.

Have patience. It will take some patience to follow through to get aging parents active again. Be prepared for moaning and groaning when he first starts walking around the block. You may hear her say that she does not enjoy pavement pounding or waving her arms up and down. But do not let her quit! Continue to encourage and remind her of how proud you are.

Review the alternatives. If your parent is not interested in being active, help him realize the choices he is faced with. Review the facts of what happens when you lead a sedentary life as opposed to an active and vital life. Remind him that we all have a choice, to challenge life or to quit and become a victim. Your parent is guaranteed premature aging once he gives in to a sedentary lifestyle. Remember that your parent's ability to function physically and with a positive attitude plays a big role in how he will finish out the best years of his life.

Enjoy the results. After six weeks of support and encouragement be ready to enjoy the results with your parent. The benefits are hard to ignore. Remind him how he felt before he started. The possibilities for exercise and activity for your parent are endless.

With her physician's approval, your parent is only limited by her imagination and creativity.

Your parent's physician can discuss with you the types of exercise program that would best meet his needs. If your parent has been active his entire life, a program of walking, swimming, bike riding, low-impact aerobics, tennis, or golf could be a place to start. His physician will guide him as to how much is enough and what is too much for his health status.

A PLAN FOR EXERCISE

WALKING

With the approval of your parent's physician, walking may be the exercise of choice. This type of exercise is a plus for most people as it requires no special equipment, no expensive clothing except a sturdy pair of shoes, and it can be done any time of the day or evening. Walking gives the health benefits of a good workout, yet has the least risk of causing injury.

Your parent should start according to the level of exercise he is used to doing. If your parent has had very little exercise, he should start by walking from one end of the house to the other or even less if this seems strenuous. As he feels stronger, encourage your parent to add to this length until he feels confident that he is ready to walk out-of-doors. If he is more comfortable inside, or if you are in a very cold, rainy, or hot climate, take advantage of enclosed malls for exercise. Many hospitals have walking clubs in the malls, and trained health care professionals keep a check on the walkers' vital signs. Check with your hospital's senior services for the programs available in your area.

If your parent has no transportation, yet does not feel safe walking alone in your neighborhood, consider a treadmill. He can watch a favorite television show or video while exercising.

LOW-IMPACT AEROBICS

Aerobic (refers to the use of oxygen) exercise causes your heart to pump oxygen to the system. This type of exercise strengthens the heart and makes it more efficient. Many senior centers offer classes in low-impact aerobics, and your parent might qualify for this healthful experience. But your parent's physician must recommend the intensity of exercise that your parent can tolerate. A physician can also explain how to monitor heart rate during any aerobic exercise. Because many elderly people have frequent wakening at night and fragmented sleep, low-impact aerobics may be the answer to feeling well. Some studies have found that aerobics may increase the amount of short-wave sleep an elderly person gets, helping her to feel more rested during the day.

WATER EXERCISES

Many communities offer water aerobics for the elderly, especially those with arthritis and joint problems. The natural buoyancy of the water helps those who are in pain or stiffened by joint problems to move their body without too much stress. These classes are usually well supervised and taught by certified instructors. Again, if your parent is not frail and moderately active, check with her physician to see if a class such as this would help get her up and moving. One added benefit of attending a class just for seniors is the opportunity for new friendships.

STRENGTH TRAINING

Resistance or strength training is becoming quite the prescription for many elderly people. This involves using one's muscles repeatedly against a mobile, weighted resistance.

One study conducted at the University of Colorado at Boulder looked at eleven men and women aged seventy to ninety-two. These elderly people—average age eighty—spent six months in an exercise program that involved pumping iron. Under close supervision they lifted weights that for them were fairly heavy. By the end of the study all the participants showed considerable gains in balance and strength—some women more than doubled their strength in certain areas.[3]

If a doctor permits, and with careful supervision, you can get your parent into strength training. Purchase some very lightweight ankle and hand weights at a sporting goods store or fill a pair of socks with dried beans—anything that will give your parent a bit of weight and resistance as he repeatedly makes a lifting motion with hands, arms, and legs. One elderly woman, who was

---

3. *Training the Body to Cure Itself* by the editors of *Prevention Magazine* (Emmaus, Pa.: Rodale Press, 1992), 10.

weakened with arthritis, told of using two cans of soup each morning to do arm lifts. "I hold one can in each hand, and put my arms down at my side," Eula Mae said. "Then I slowly lift each arm ten times." Eula found that her total strength increased to the point that she could even do more housework and gardening.

YOGA

Yoga is a helpful exercise to many seniors. Dr. Dean Ornish, author of *Dr. Dean Ornish's Program for Reversing Heart Disease,* uses yoga in his cardiac research programs. Using modified poses, yoga can be used by most people, even those in wheelchairs. It can help them relax and become more flexible, and, depending on the difficulty, it can even build muscle strength like weight training.

Check with your Area Agency on Aging for a yoga class just for seniors, or look at a nearby video store for a beginner's lesson. Again, never start your parent on an exercise routine until he has had a thorough medical evaluation and the positive consent of the physician. When you have permission, make sure your parent receives proper instruction and observation.

PHYSICAL THERAPY

Physical therapy is about motion—improving it, restoring it, encouraging it. People who can benefit from physical therapy include those with a sports injury or muscle pain, stroke or burn patients, people who have had a heart attack, or anyone who wants to improve his or her physical conditioning.[4]

You will want to get a physician's recommendation for your parent to begin physical therapy. But for elderly adults who have chronic health problems that deprive them of an active lifestyle, physical therapy is the safe and healthful way to keep them limber, flexible, and strong.

PROCEED WITH CAUTION

Remember that as we age, we lose our "meter" for thirst. It is very important to make sure that your parent gets plenty of fluids if he is exercising. Check with your parent's physician about how much liquid your parent needs daily as well as when he exercises.

---

4. Ibid., 379.

Some alternatives to get much-needed fluids include supplementing the diet with gelatin or frozen fruit bars after exercising.

ADULT EDUCATION

Many seniors tell of activities they always "wanted to do if only they could just find the time." Well, now is the time to encourage your parent to get involved.

The local adult education program in your town offers many programs that teach new skills and hobbies and provide opportunities to meet other seniors. Your parent can make new friends, expand her horizons, and possibly start a second career as she becomes an "expert" in a new skill.

SENIOR CLUBS

Thousands of groups of senior adults meet across the country as they enjoy doing things together. There are travel clubs, exercise groups, dance clubs like square dancing and ballroom dancing, hiking groups, bird watching clubs, garden clubs, walking groups, and more. Check with your Area Agency on Aging.

CONTINUING EDUCATION

Senior adults can take advantage of continuing education. Many community colleges and universities allow mature adults to audit classes at little or no cost. Check into a degree program for your parent, if he wants to obtain a college diploma during retirement and see if he can get credit for "life experiences." The opportunities are many.

ELDERHOSTEL

Elderhostel is a wonderful educational experience just for older adults who want to continue to expand their horizons and to develop new interests and enthusiasms. Elderhostel is designed for seniors who want to visit new places and stimulate their imagination. Participants can enjoy inexpensive, short-term programs at educational institutions around the world. The senior adult lives on the college campus while attending class and can get involved in the many cultural and recreational activities on that campus.

(Write for a catalog from Elderhostel, 75 Federal St., Boston, MA, 02110.)

VOLUNTEER TO SERVE

The worst thing that people can do is to center only on themselves. The retirement years are an outstanding time to get involved with others—a time when seniors are "liberated to serve." One way is to teach or volunteer in the local church or public school system. Other ways to get involved include your community hospital, religious groups, charitable organizations, day care centers, or other nonprofit groups such as the American Cancer Society or American Heart Association.

The ideas for activity are endless for service and activity. You can help your parent set new goals for her life. Ask, "If you could do anything in the world, what would it be? Where would you go? What would you see? Who would you meet?" Help him to zero in on specific areas of interest, and then challenge him to begin an active senior lifestyle to pursue these dreams. New goals might include the following:

- making new friends

- starting a mid-week group for seniors at church

- volunteering to cook meals for the youth at church

- helping in the pediatric ward at a local hospital

- teaching children with learning disabilities

- writing an autobiography

- starting a garden

- playing golf with friends

- enjoying the outdoors while boating and fishing

- assisting a neighbor who is shut-in

- getting to know grandchildren more intimately

- traveling with friends

- learning how to paint, sew, do woodwork, or write

- learning a musical instrument

- being a surrogate grandparent for a child in the neighborhood or church

- looking up old high school friends

- researching the family's genealogy

- starting a part-time career

- redecorating the home

SHOPPING

Your parent should be encouraged to get out and go shopping, whether to the grocery store or the local mall. Shopping as a form of activity adds diversity to a daily exercise routine.

She can go with a friend and participate in mall exercise programs sponsored by wellness centers and then spend the morning browsing through the stores. Be sure your parent wears comfortable shoes and a hip-pack that buckles around the waist to carry money and personal items.

TRAVEL

Many elderly adults worry that travel at their age may be dangerous. One seventy-two-year-old woman with osteoarthritis canceled a trip to see her new granddaughter because of a fear of injury.

Another seventy-one-year-old gentleman told his grandson he could not attend his wedding for fear of "walking down the aisle and falling." Still another elderly woman missed the baptism of her twin great-grandchildren because she was afraid that she could not keep up with "the busyness of the event."

While these personal fears may seem real, they are not valid. For most elderly people who are able to move reasonably well and who are in good health, travel can be that perfect form of exercise and activity that not only keeps the body moving but also stimulates the mind and broadens horizons. Being older does not mean that your parent needs less exercise; rather, at that stage in life exercise and activity, including travel, become most vital for physical and mental well-being.

Continue exercising. Do not forget that exercise keeps your parent flexible and limber and keeps the muscles strong. If he is taking a long trip in a car, remind him to stop frequently. Have her walk around while stretching arms and legs. The range of motion exercises given in this chapter are perfect for preventing stiffness and pain while traveling.

During travel on an airplane, your parent may find that the pain and stiffness becomes worse after sitting in one position for a while. This can be controlled by walking up and down the aisle of the plane for five to ten minutes each hour. This can help prevent stiffness and fatigue. Also, it is better to choose a nonstop flight so your parent does not have to experience lengthy layovers at strange airports.

Choose a hotel that meets his needs. Many hotels now have heated swimming pools or whirlpools. Remember, your parent must continue to exercise away from home in order to remain flexible and strong during the trip.

If your parent is in a wheelchair, make certain that the hotel has wheelchair ramps to make it accessible. You may want to ask about rooms with grab bars in the bathroom, toilet, or other areas.

Remember other tips to help. While at the destination, remind your parent not to plan a schedule too full of activities. The amount of sightseeing or business should be reasonable for the time available. If your parent is with a tour group, make sure it is with seniors his age so the leader understands the necessity of rest along with sightseeing. If your parent becomes too tired while traveling, he could need to miss some portions of the tour to rest and recover, before resuming full activities later. In other words, your parent should pace his activities so that he does not wear out too soon. If he does this, he will find that he can accomplish the same amount, but will not have to suffer pain, stiffness, and fatigue.

Think protection. When your parent is traveling, she will need to protect her back and joints to avoid injury. When sightseeing, she should avoid carrying heavy equipment, cameras, suitcases, or bags. These all take a toll on the back and joints and can add to tiredness long before the day is finished. If walking is too tiring or causes pain, she should not hesitate to rent a wheelchair or cart. Then she will be able to keep up with everyone else.

There are many more examples of smart ways to travel so that your parent can get around to and do many activities, but still not cause severe pain, stiffness, and fatigue. But the important goal is to get your parent out and into the world so the mind and body receives the much needed stimulation to stay fit and alert.[5]

Exercise for the Frail Elderly

Your parent's physician will decide what activities are appropriate for your parent. If your parent is frail and does not have much energy, you may have to do some daily tasks for your parent so that he may have energy for socializing and mental stimulation. But it is also important to let your parent do as many personal care activities as he can for his self-esteem.

Tips on Assisting the Frail Elderly

The frail elderly can move around more, if you help them learn some personal care and grooming tips. These suggestions can help the frail elderly perform personal care for independence and range of motion activity.

Eating. Mealtime can be made easier with a few accommodations to assist your parent in the process. If your parent is able to come to the table, this is best for social reasons. If he is in a wheelchair, a lap board can be used as well as the table. Utensils with built-up handles will allow for a better grip for weak hands; cylindrical foam padding can be purchased at medical supply stores for this purpose. Bicycle rubber grips can also be used as well (place each piece over the handle and cut at the end). Angled or swiveled utensils help those who have trouble moving the wrists and forearm. If reach is limited, extension handles can alleviate this problem. Lightweight mugs with large handles can be purchased for those with grip problems. Covered cups and mugs can give protection from spills, and straws are also a good idea for those with limited motion. Your local medical supply store can show you devices that will meet your parent's special needs.

Bathing. Frail elderly can use a terry cloth mitt, long-handled brush or sponge, soap on a rope, skid-proof mat in bathtub, handheld shower head, a skid-proof stool with a back to sit on, grab bars, and a terry cloth robe to dry himself and put on after the bath. A bath rack that fits across the tub can hold bath items to assist in cleaning. A "toe cleaner" can be made out of a yardstick with

---

5. Harris H. McIlwain, et al., *Winning with Osteoporosis,* 143.

a cotton sock slipped over the end and secured with a rubber band. This keeps your parent from falling when leaning over to clean his feet. Soaking the nails before trimming makes the process easier. Use long nail clippers for ease in holding for weak grips. A battery-operated manicure kit is also available.

Dental Care. Show your parent how to use a battery operated toothbrush or how to squeeze toothpaste by putting the tube between the knees. The new pump toothpaste is also easier to use than the squeeze type.

Grooming. If the grasp is weak, purchase an electric razor. Women can use a cream hair remover and a roll on deodorant. They should keep their hair short or permed to keep grooming simple. Velcro attached to a flat brush can wrap around the hand to assist your parent if she is weak.

Toileting. Use an elevated toilet set or bedside commode. Install grab bars along the side of the toilet, and provide long-handled tongs to hold tissue for wiping.

Clothing. Clothing must be well thought out and include light weight pieces that are easy to slip off and on. These should clasp with Velcro, if possible. Your parent should slip the weakened arm into clothing first, use the stronger arm to pull the clothing on, and then button or Velcro. There are also pincher devices for hose or socks, elastic waist pants, slip on shoes with elastic laces, and long-handled shoe horns. The best clothing for women are wrap-around skirts, dresses, jumpers that hook with Velcro instead of zippers or buttons; women should use bras that open from the front. Men's clothing also should have Velcro instead of zippers. Ponchos that slip over the head and shoulders can be worn for cold weather or rain.

HOME CHORES FOR THE FRAIL ELDERLY

Equally important to the movements with personal care are chores around the home that can keep your parent active and mobile:

Laundry. Purchase a waist-high laundry basket on wheels. Your parent can fold his clothes while sitting or if bedridden, have him use a lapboard and fold while in bed.

Ironing. If your parent is able to iron, she can do this by sitting at the ironing board.

Sweeping. Have your parent use an electric broom or a broom and long-handled dust pan.

Washing Dishes. Place a rubber mat in the bottom of the sink to prevent breakage, or have your parent use plastic cups and dishes (lightweight and unbreakable). If one hand or arm is disabled, place the dishrack near the arm that is functional.

Preparing Meals. Keep meals simple. Have your parent gather all items needed, and sit at the table to make salad, cut up meat, or chop vegetables. This will prevent unnecessary fatigue. Keep most frequently used spices on a Lazy Susan on the table. A bar stool can be pulled up to the counter or sink to work in this area. Because of difficulty in lifting, encourage the frail elderly to purchase small containers of milk, juice, and soda, or pour the liquid into smaller containers for them. A pot with a colander inside for foods that must be drained can prevent serious burns. An electric skillet may be easier to use if using the stove is difficult.

General Cleaning. Use a waist-level basket on wheels to move supplies from room to room or to keep items needed in each room. Your parent can also put cleaning supplies in a carrier that hooks onto a walker or wheelchair or carry small items in pockets of an apron.

Making Beds. Purchase oversized flat sheets, and sew long pieces of elastic (about twelve inches long) across each corner. Lay the sheet on the bed. Taking a long-handled paddle, have your parent pull elastic over corners of the mattress, then take the paddle and push the remaining sheet under the mattress. Also use oversized pillowcases as they are easier to change.

Gardening. Have your parent sit on a stool while working, and remind him to get up and walk around regularly to keep from getting stiff.

Talking on the Telephone. Some telephones are voice activated for bedridden persons. Some phones have an oversized dial (with large numbers) that the person can dial using an eraser of a pencil. Others have an automatic dial for the most commonly called numbers. You can also purchase a lightweight phone or one with a shoulder support to free up the hands or to use if her arms cannot be used. Keep paper and pens by the phone for notes or use a daily calendar for keeping track of appointments and messages.

Reading. You can get large print books from the library; books on tape are also available at most department stores as well as libraries. A book holder can help if your parent is weak. A rubber thumb can be purchased at an office supply store to assist those with arthritis or weak hands in turning pages. A parent who is homebound because of stroke or visual impairment can qualify for the Talking Books program of the Library of Congress. With referral by a physician, this program will deliver records and cassettes of books and magazines at no charge. Ask your local librarian for an application. (Look in Appendix B for information on tapes for the disabled and visually impaired.)

Watching Television and VCRs. Be sure your parent has a remote control. If he is hard of hearing, a device can be attached to the television to enhance the sound (check with a hearing specialist). You can rent videos; and documentaries on travel, different cultures, or animals are also available at video stores.

Writing. Have supplies by the bed or chair such as a pen, paper, stamps, cards, typewriter, computer, cassette recorder for ideas and messages, and notes for telephone messages. A clipboard, lap board, or beanbag lap desk is great for those who are weak or bedridden. Triangular grips (available in the school supply section of the store) for pencils or pens give a better grip for weak fingers.

WHEELCHAIRS AND ACTIVITY

Even if your parent is confined to a wheelchair, there are creative ways to keep your parent active. Try to use the personal care suggestions listed above, and check with his physician for special limitations prior to starting a range of motion exercise program.

All aging adults, including bedridden patients, need to follow a regime of range of motion exercises as well as daily activities. The physician can recommend the type that would best meet your parent's needs. Exercises such as raising the head, turning the head, shoulder shrug, arms over head, arm circle, hand, finger rotation, and leg raise can help strengthen muscles and increase mobility.

EXERCISES FOR INCREASED MOBILITY

Exercises for mobility are most effective when done properly. You can have your parent learn specific exercises from a qualified physical therapist or physician. Be sure to check with your parent's physician to get approval on any exercises you choose and to design a program with your parent's needs in mind.

LEARN RANGE OF MOTION EXERCISES

You can do range of motion exercises with your parent, if she has the doctor's approval. If your parent is bedridden or in a wheelchair, adapt so there is some movement.

Range of motion exercises involve taking each part of the body, starting at the head, and moving it through a comfortable range of motion. You will move the head slowly, with smooth motions, then proceed to the shoulders, arms, hands, fingers, and other areas. If you are not sure how to do this correctly, ask a physical therapist for an exact plan to meet your parent's needs.

Many range of motion exercises can be done while sitting in a chair at home, with no special equipment. They can also be done in a car, in an airplane, or in a hotel room when traveling.

With a doctor's approval, your parent should start by doing one or two of these exercises once or twice each day. He can gradually increase up to five, then ten of each exercise once or twice each day. If your parent's pain worsens, or if he feels dizziness or shortness of breath when exercising, stop until consulting the doctor.

STRENGTHEN MUSCLES TO AVOID FALLS

Falls are common when frail elderly try to sit down or get out of a chair, go up and down the stairs, or walk outside to get the mail. It makes sense to strengthen the muscles that are used for these activities to limit the chances for a fall due to muscle weakness.

A few exercises can be done to help strengthen the muscles in the legs to reduce the chance of falling. Check with your parent's physician, and see if these would benefit your parent to strengthen his legs.

Sitting Down. To reduce the risk of falls and hip fractures, make sure your parent avoids any chair or couch that puts the hips lower than the knees. To build strength, have your parent back up to a firm chair with his arms as if getting ready to sit down.

Tell your parent to place the back of his legs against the chair and rest his hands on the armrest without putting any weight on his arms. Have him try to sit without using his arms for support, but use arms if feeling weak. Try this two times and increase as the doctor approves. This exercise helps to strengthen the legs, giving aging adults more confidence against falls.

Stairs. Have your parent put his arm on the banister that is on the side of his strongest leg. Holding onto the banister, he should step up with the strongest leg and then drag the other leg up to meet it. Your parent should have good eye contact at the place he is going to step. Have him do the same procedure in stepping back down, holding on with the arm on the side of the strongest leg and stepping with the strongest leg. See if the physician feels this would strengthen your parent's legs, and always be there with him to prevent falls.

Bed. When your parent awakens, ask her to wait a few moments to orient herself to the surroundings. She should move her arms and legs a little, sit up slowly, and then swing her legs off the side of the bed. She should sit for a moment and make sure she doesn't feel dizzy. If she does, she should wait until she feels she can safely stand. With her legs leaning against the bed, she can rise slowly using her legs not arms. This strengthens the legs. Be there to steady your parent, and, again, be sure your parent's physician approves.

CAN YOUR PARENT MEET THE CHALLENGE?

Make a chart similar to the ones shown below, and list the various activities your parent can do. Have your parent checkmark the actual activities or exercises she does each week. If she is very active, she may tell you that she is also "very tired." But look beyond what she says. Does she feel more positive? Does she hurt less from joint pain? Is she sleeping sounder? Reward your parent with hugs, and praise her for taking charge of her health.

Weekly Challenge Chart—Activities

	M	T	W	TH	F	S	S
Worship services							
Volunteer work							
Women's (men's) group							
Sunday School							
Grandchild's activity (sports, recital, other)							
Senior center							
Meal program							

Weekly Challenge Chart—Activities (Continued)

Hobby classes							
Church night supper							
Bible study							
Concert							
Adult day care							
Social clubs							

Weekly Challenge Chart—Exercises

	M	T	W	TH	F	S	S	M
Daily walk								
Yoga								
Household chores								
Gardening (outdoor or indoor)								
Stretching exercises								
Range of motion exercises								
Water aerobics								
Low impact aerobics								
Strength training								

The benefits of activity and exercise for the elderly are numerous. Now it is time to take this knowledge and do something with it. You and your parent will have a better sense of self-worth once you get started.

8

NUTRITION AND YOUR PARENT'S HEALTH

"You are what you eat." How many times did Mom or Dad remind you of this growing up? What your parent told you is true as studies have proven that many common diseases can be related to the foods we eat each day. For example, a diet high in sodium can raise blood pressure levels in sensitive people, increasing the risk of heart disease. A diet high in fat can lead to obesity, some types of cancer, and heart attack. The foods we eat do influence every part of our health and well-being.

Regardless of your parent's health status, this chapter will help. Nutritional education is important for everyone, especially those in their senior years. Instead of a quick nutritional fix for enhancing your parent's health, you need to understand which nutrients are important for elderly adults, how healthful foods play a role in the management of certain problems common to them, and how simple steps can be taken right now through diet to boost your parent's energy, immunity, and wellness.

Discuss the information in this chapter with your parent. Together, meet with a physician or dietitian and plan a healthful diet that meets his specific physical needs and increases well-being. If your parent is unable to prepare his own foods, see chapter 4 for ideas on obtaining home care food services.

In a recent study by the National Council on Aging, the American Dietetic Association, and the American Academy of Family Physicians, nutritional intake of those over sixty-five was found inadequate. This study, the National Nutrition Screening Initiative, found that 20 percent of Americans over the age of sixty-five suffer from poor nutrition. Also 85 percent of senior Americans were found to have one or more chronic conditions, such as depression, diabetes, or hypertension, which require nutrition intervention and possibly special foods. Furthermore, about one third of older Americans skip meals almost every day, and almost one half of older Americans take medications that suppress appetite. All these findings point to one important fact: Those over sixty-five are at risk for poor nutrition for a variety of reasons.

- Many take several medications.

- Many have inadequate funding to purchase the food they need.

- Many require a special diet for an illness or a condition.

- Some wear poor fitting dentures or have poor dental health.

- Many eat less than three meals a day.

- Some have physical ailments, which make them unable to shop, cook, or feed themselves.

- Many consume few perishables like fresh fruits and vegetables or milk products.

- Many live alone and eat meals alone.

NUTRITION GUIDELINES AFTER SIXTY-FIVE

Because of the many factors that influence the diet of older Americans, seniors can easily become at risk for nutrient deficiencies. But, with proper understanding of a healthful diet for mature adults, these deficiencies can often be remedied by including food sources of the following nutrients. Go over the following list of nutrients with your parent to understand their importance.

Beta-carotene is the storage form of vitamin A. Vitamin A is needed by the body to provide resistance to infection, to prevent night blindness, and to maintain the health of the mucous membranes. This vitamin is found in some fruits and vegetables.

Symptoms of vitamin A deficiency are seldom seen in the United States unless the diet of the older American lacks a variety of fruits and vegetables. Vitamin A is readily available in foods such as cantaloupe, carrots, greens, peaches, spinach, and sweet potatoes or in vitamin supplements.

Calcium is necessary for maintaining strong bones. A deficiency of calcium can contribute to osteoporosis and muscle weakness (see chap. 2 for more on osteoporosis and the elderly). Women after menopause are at the highest risk for bone loss. Good sources of calcium include lowfat milk, lowfat cheese, lowfat yogurt, and pudding (see the chart below for other ways to add calcium to your parent's diet). If your parent has a lactose intolerance to dairy products, you should buy lactose-free milk or use the powdered lactase product in milk.

Vitamin D enhances the absorption of calcium. Therefore, sun exposure, which allows the body to make vitamin D, and drinking vitamin D fortified milk can be helpful. Or, your parent can add a calcium supplement.

Sources of Calcium		
Food	Amount	Milligrams
Cheese, cheddar	1 ounce	204
Cheese, part-skim mozzarella	1 ounce	183
Collard greens, cooked	1/2 cup	152
Milk, skim	1 cup	302
Salmon, fresh	3 ounces	258
Sardines, Pacific, canned	3 ounces	260
Yogurt, lowfat	1 cup	325

Folic acid is one of the B-complex vitamins. It functions in the body's cell growth and assists in keeping nerve and brain cells from deteriorating. A lack of this important vitamin may cause instances of memory loss that may be mistaken for dementia in the elderly. Good sources of folic acid include broccoli, orange juice, leafy green vegetables, beans, and grains.

Potassium deficiency may be common in older Americans, caused by a diet low in fruits, vegetables, and milk. Medications like some diuretics can cause an excessive loss of potassium in the urine and result in a deficiency. Poor diabetic control or prolonged vomiting and diarrhea can also produce a potassium deficiency. Symptoms of a potassium deficiency include weakness, nausea, poor appetite, and confusion. Your parent can have good sources of potassium by eating bananas, citrus fruits, cantaloupes, tomatoes, dried fruit, greens, and potatoes regularly.

Vitamin B_6 is needed by the body to use the food we eat and to help with red blood cell production. A lack of vitamin B_6 may cause one form of anemia and irritability. Good sources of vitamin B_6 include bananas, pork, beef liver, and egg yolks.

Vitamin B_{12} also is vital to keep nerve and brain cells from deteriorating, and a deficiency can cause memory loss. Good sources of vitamin B_{12} include liver, beef, eggs, milk, and shellfish.

Vitamin C deficiency may cause bruising, weakness, gingivitis, and bleeding gums. A diet inadequate in fruits and vegetables, characteristic of the diet of the elderly, can lead to low blood levels of vitamin C. Some evidence suggests that vitamin C might slow the progression of cataracts also. Good sources of vitamin C are citrus fruits, strawberries, greens, and tomatoes or vitamin supplements.

Vitamin E is important to the body for the maintenance of the cell membranes. Vitamin E is readily available in vegetable oils.

Vitamins E, C, and beta-carotene are the antioxidant nutrients. Antioxidants are substances in the body that build the body's defenses against free radicals. Free radicals from chemical reactions in the body might contribute to such problems as heart disease and atherosclerosis. Adequate intakes of vitamin E, C, and beta-carotene are recommended from diet or supplements.

PROVIDE AN ADEQUATE DAILY DIET

A balanced daily diet that includes a variety of foods should be the primary method of obtaining all the essential nutrients for the elderly. Depending on your parent's specific problems, he may need more or less food than is written. You should check with your parent's doctor to see if additional vitamin or mineral supplements are needed and if the following diet would meet your parent's specific health needs.

Suggestions for a Geriatric Diet		
Food Group	Servings	Serving Size
Eggs, lean meat, poultry, fish and beans	2 to 3 per day	2 to 3 ounces
Lowfat milk, cheese, and yogurt	3 per day	1 cup or 1 ounce
Grains, breads, and cereals	6 to 11 per day (depending on calorie needs)	1/2 cup, one slice, or one ounce
Fruits and Vegetables	2 to 4 fruits and 3 to 5 vegetables per day	1 piece fruit, 1/2 to 1 cup

FOLLOW THE U.S. DIETARY GUIDELINES

The menu suggestions below follow the U.S. Dietary Guidelines recommended by the Department of Agriculture and the U.S. Department of Health and Human Services. Go over these recommendations with your parent and write down suggestions to enhance your parent's daily menus.

Your parent needs to include a variety of foods in his diet. His needs for nutrients, with the exception of needing fewer calories, do not differ from adults of all ages. Therefore, foods in the diet should be chosen carefully, limiting the calories contributed from fat and sugar.

Your parent's diet should be low in sugar as it contributes calories but has little nutritional value. Sugar may be found in many

Breakfast
whole grain cereal with lowfat milk, egg, or egg substitute
whole-grain bread with margarine
whole fruit or fruit juice
coffee or hot tea

Lunch
meat, beans, or cheese
cooked vegetable or raw vegetables or salad with lowfat dressing
whole-grain bread with margarine or mayonnaise for sandwich
whole fruit
lowfat milk

Dinner
meat, beans, or cheese
cooked vegetable or raw vegetables or salad with lowfat dressing
starch such as potato, pasta, or rice
whole fruit salad or fruit juice
whole-grain bread with margarine
lowfat milk
light dessert

food products. To help your parent avoid sugar encourage these suggestions:

- Read the ingredients of the food product to determine the sugar content. If possible, select an alternate product without sugar. For example, select a water-packed can of fruit over one packed in syrup.

- Use products sweetened with nonnutritive sweeteners (calorie-free) like aspartame (Equal™) or saccharine (Sweet-n-Low™).

- Select sugar-free or low sugar cereals.

Your parent's diet should be low in saturated fat, by including lowfat and fat-free milk products and lean meats. To help your parent reduce fat and cholesterol in the diet, encourage the following suggestions:

- Buy lean meat and trim the visible fat. Drain and discard the fat cooked out of the meat.

- Buy more fish, poultry without skin, and veal, as each is lower in fat than beef, pork, and lamb.

- Limit eggs to two to three per week. Substitute two egg whites for each egg yolk in cooking and baking.

- Substitute whole milk products with skim milk or lower fat milk counterparts.

- Cook with polyunsaturated(corn, safflower, or sunflower) or monounsaturated (olive or canola) oils. A polyunsaturated fat margarine should be used (corn or safflower oil are listed first in the ingredients list) instead of lard, butter, or shortening. Margarine with monounsaturated (canola) fat is fine too.

- Use monounsaturated oil like olive oil in salad dressings, pasta, and vegetable salads.

- Use vegetable protein sources instead of meat on occasion. For example, one cup of cooked dried beans or peas have about as much protein as a two- or three-ounce serving of cooked meat, but much less fat. Combine the beans with rice or wheat bread to make the protein equivalent to meat protein.

- Recommend cooking methods that do not require fat like boiling, broiling, baking, microwaving, roasting, and stewing. Stir frying is acceptable if using only a small amount of polyunsaturated or monounsaturated fat oil.

- Limit intake of regular luncheon meat, hot dogs, and sausage. Reduced fat meat products are available.

Your parent's diet should avoid excess salt, but allow the use of salt for taste. Salt can be reduced in the diet by limiting salty foods, such as canned and processed foods. To help your parent avoid a high salt/sodium intake encourage the following suggestions:

- Avoid excessive amounts of sodium by using fresh, frozen, or no-salt-added canned vegetables.

- Use fresh meats, fish, chicken instead of canned or processed meat like luncheon meat (ham, bologna, bacon, sausage).

- Avoid the use of convenience box mixes (macaroni and cheese, scalloped potatoes, dressing mixes) and frozen convenience foods (TV dinners, vegetables in white or cheese sauces, frozen potato products). Even some low-calorie frozen dinners are high in sodium and should be used cautiously.

- Use herbs, commercial salt-free seasonings, salt substitutes, lemon juice, or vinegar to flavor foods.

- Eat fast foods infrequently or choose the salad bar.

- Use creative alternatives instead of high-fat foods.

Lean Choice Substitutions

If currently using	Try these alternatives
Butter	Reduced calorie corn oil or margarine
Cheese	Lowfat cheese
Ground beef	Ground round, ground sirloin, ground turkey
Luncheon meat	Lowfat luncheon meat
Mayonnaise	Reduced calorie mayonnaise
Oil	Vegetable oil cooking spray
Salad dressing	Oil free or reduced calorie salad dressing
Sour cream	No fat or lowfat sour cream

Your parent also should increase fiber in diet, as tolerated. (See chart later in this chapter.) A liberal fluid intake is recommended to help with bowel function and prevent dehydration. Ask your parent's physician for the amount of fluids needed each day.

HEALTHY KITCHEN CHECKLIST

Making the best food choices is important when calorie or fat limitations are given. The following healthy kitchen checklist will show your parent which food items are healthful and which ones should be limited or even avoided.

Healthy Kitchen Checklist

Yes	No
Skim or 1% milk	Whole milk
Part-skim cheeses—mozzarella, ricotta	Cheeses made with whole milk
Reduced fat cheeses (less than 5 grams of fat per ounce)	
Lowfat cottage cheese	
Lowfat yogurt	
Fresh fruits, fruits canned in their own juices, unsweetened fruit juice, dried fruits	Sugar coated fruits and fruit fillings, canned fruits in syrup
Raw vegetables, steamed vegetables, or vegetables cooked crisp	Vegetables cooked soft or cooked with meat fat
Skinless poultry, fish, very lean cuts of red meat, reduced fat luncheon meats (less than 5 grams of fat per ounce)	Commercial sausage, bacon, regular luncheon meat, hot dogs, fat marbled red meats
Whole grain bread and cereal products, crackers with unsalted tops, unsalted popcorn	White bread, refined breakfast cereals (low fiber), salted or flavored crackers, popcorn, or nuts
Unsaturated vegetable oils, (corn, safflower, sunflower, soybean, olive), margarines made with liquid corn oil or safflower oil	Excessive amounts of saturated fat (animal fats, shortening, hydrogenated fats)

Healthy Kitchen Checklist (Continued)

Yes	No
Commercial egg substitute, egg whites	Whole egg, egg yolk
Vegetable oil based salad dressings, low calorie or oil-free salad dressing	Creamy or cheesy salad dressings (sour cream cheese-based dressings)
Fruit juice popsicles, sherbet, angel food cake, bran muffins	Commercial baked goods (pies, cakes, cookies), packaged cookies containing palm, coconut or hydrogenated oils.

THE CHANGES OF AGING

Many physical changes accompany aging which often affect how people eat. Some mature adults find that food no longer has an appeal or that they cannot eat the same food because of a health problem; therefore, they lose interest in food. But when elderly adults do not eat properly, their physical and mental well-being will suffer.

Help your parent learn to prepare healthful foods that please the tastes, depending on your parent's sense of smell, ability to chew, and other factors.

DIMINISHED SENSE OF TASTE AND SMELL

Your parent may have noticed that aging has caused the loss of the sense of taste. The sense of smell also diminishes with aging, and this affects taste. The sense of smell may be up to ten times less sensitive in the elderly than in younger people. Here are some suggestions on how to make foods for mature adults taste better:

- Give variety on the dinner plate. The sense of smell adapts to the smell of a food within a few seconds. Therefore, the first bite of a new food gives the largest sensation of smell and consequently of taste. By alternating bites of various foods on the plate, the meal tastes better.

- Vary the texture and temperature of the foods on the dinner plate. Include foods of varied textures and consistencies with some hot and some cold foods.

- Experiment with herbs and spices in cooking. Fresh herbs are more potent than dried ones.

- Ask your parent's physician if any medications may interfere with appetite or alter taste.

CHEWING DIFFICULTIES

Major factors that put older persons at nutritional risk are poor dental health or ill-fitting dentures. Chewing difficulties can limit your parent's dietary intake and lead to nutrient deficiencies.

The following suggestions may help with chewing difficulties:

- Moisten foods with gravies and sauces to make them easier to chew.

- Chop, grate, or blenderize foods if your parent has no teeth. A liquid or pudding supplement several times per day can provide almost complete nutrition.

- Soak foods in liquid for a more tender texture. You can also braise or stew meats to tenderize.

- Use moist foods, casseroles, macaroni and cheese, yogurt, and cottage cheese for protein choices.

WEIGHT LOSS

Frequently, following hospitalization or a homebound illness, you may find that your parent has experienced significant weight loss. Weight loss of five percent or more of body weight should prompt some dietary changes. Here are some suggestions to boost the protein and calorie intake of older persons:

- Provide your parent with small, frequent meals to encourage eating. Keep favorite snack foods in stock and provide them throughout the day.

- Save favorite foods for meals when the appetite is poorest.

- If your parent does not like hot meats, try cold meat salads (turkey, chicken, tuna, or egg salad) to provide protein. Luncheon meats, cheese, deviled eggs, milkshakes, puddings, and custards also provide protein and are often readily received by the weak older person.

- Add powdered milk to milkshakes, puddings, custards, and casseroles to increase their protein and calorie content.

- Fortify whole milk by adding one cup of dry milk to one quart of fluid milk. This doubles the protein content of the milk.

- If meat is tolerated, marinate it in a variety of spices to enhance flavor. Use sugar and salt (if allowed by physician) as desired or try a marinade of fruit juice.

- Use extra margarine to add fat calories to food. Sour cream, cream cheese, and whipped cream, while high in saturated fat, are high in calories, so use them liberally in the diet of an older person with weight loss.

- Foods high in carbohydrates are often readily consumed and can add calories to the diet. Include popsicles, jelly, jam, honey, flavored gelatin, marshmallows, and other candies besides the liberal geriatric diet.

If your parent continues to lose weight, a nutritional supplement should be considered. Nutritional supplements can boost the calories and protein in the diet of an older person who has a poor appetite and undesired weight loss. The list below includes those supplements free of the milk carbohydrate lactose that may cause diarrhea and gas in those who are lactose intolerant. Those supplements that contain milk are also listed. Be sure to check with your parent's physician or dietitian to see if supplementation is warranted.

In choosing a nutritional supplement, you need to consider individual taste and economics. Most of these supplements can be found in the local pharmacy or can be ordered upon request. Instant breakfast mixes (found in grocery stores) are by far the least expensive supplements; however, they are mixed with milk and therefore contain lactose. All supplements may be more appealing if mixed with ice cream or fruit. Most supplements are available in liquid form (like a milkshake) and pudding. The powder mixes are usually less expensive even though they may be more time consuming to make.

Nutritional Supplements	
Product	Company
Boost™ (liquid)	
Ensure™ (a liquid)	Ross
Ensure™ Plus (a liquid)	Ross
Enrich™ (a liquid)	Ross
Resource™ (a powder)	Sandoz
Sustacal™ (a liquid)	Mead Johnson
Sustacal High Calorie™ (a liquid)	Mead Johnson
Supplements containing milk	
Meritene™ (a liquid or powder)	Sandoz
Sustacal™ (mix with milk)	Mead Johnson
Sustagen™ (mix with milk)	Mead Johnson
Instant breakfast™ (mix with milk)	Carnation

NUTRITIONAL PROBLEMS

The following conditions and diseases are very common among elderly people, even healthy mature adults. Many of these problems can be affected by improper nutrition. If you understand how nutrition plays a role in your parent's healing, you can recommend the proper foods to enhance health.

Diverticulosis. As many as half of all Americans over the age of sixty-five have a condition called diverticulosis. People with diverticulosis may develop symptoms such as bloating, gas, nausea, and constipation. More severe abdominal pain, fever, nausea, and constipation may indicate the presence of infection or a condition called *diverticulitis.*

The major step for prevention of diverticulosis in older Americans is to eat more fiber. (Fiber is a combination of plant materials that resist digestion.) Increased fiber in the diet produces a softer and bulkier stool that is easier to pass and puts less pressure on the intestinal wall. Foods high in fiber include whole grain bread and cereal products, especially those containing wheat bran.

Raw fruits and vegetables with the peels can also add fiber to the diet. To increase the fiber in meals and snacks, add a teaspoon or two of wheat germ or use 100 percent bran cereal.

Another dietary change includes drinking plenty of fluid every day which should aid the action of the fiber in making the stool softer and preventing constipation and straining during a bowel movement. A word of caution: Nuts and foods with seeds may inflame the diverticula by getting caught inside them; therefore, these foods should be avoided or chewed well.

Constipation. Each year, two and one half million Americans visit their physician for treatment of constipation. Those over sixty-five are more inclined to have this problem. The treatment and prevention of constipation involves adding more fiber and fluid to the diet. The American Dietetic Association recommends that older Americans eat twenty to thirty-five grams of fiber a day to get the health benefits fiber has to offer. Most Americans consume on an average just twelve grams of fiber per day. The increased level of fiber should be introduced slowly, and the amount can be reduced if diarrhea or pain from gas persists.

To end constipation, encourage your parent to use the insoluble fiber found in whole grain foods, wheat bran, and in some vegetables. For example, prunes are not only a good source of fiber, but they also contain a substance that stimulates the colon to pass stool.

Additional suggestions for the treatment and prevention of constipation include the following:

- Encourage your parent to get plenty of exercise (see chap. 7). Short, brisk walks during the day can help with regularity.

- Encourage your parent to drink a hot cup of coffee, tea, or water early in the morning to stimulate the colon and promote a bowel movement.

A nutritional supplement or medication may contribute to constipation. Some forms of iron and calcium supplements can cause constipation, and medications such as some antacids, antihistamines, diuretics, and some heart medications can also cause constipation. Consult your parent's physician to see if this is the cause of the bowel problem.

Fiber Content of Selected Foods

Food	Amount	Grams
bran muffin	1 average	3
whole wheat	1 slice	2
bran flakes	1 ounce	4
100% Bran™	1 ounce	10
raisin bran	1 ounce	3.5–4
dried prunes, medium	3	4
raisins	2 Tbs.	1.2
apple (with skin)	1 medium	3
cantaloupe, cubes	1 cup	2
grapefruit	1/2 medium	2.5
orange	1 medium	2
pear, raw	1 medium	2.8
strawberries, raw	1 1/4 cup	6.5
beans, green	1/2 cup	1.5
broccoli, cooked	1/2 cup	1.1
cabbage, cooked	1/2 cup	1.5
carrots, cooked	1/2 cup	1.4
carrots, raw	1 medium	3.7
cauliflower, cooked	1/2 cup	1.2
cauliflower, raw	1 cup	1.8
kale, cooked	1/2 cup	2
kidney beans, cooked	7 1/2 cup	7
peas, cooked	1/2 cup	4
potato, baked	1 with skin	3.5
summer squash	1/2 cup	2.2

Hemorrhoids. More than half of all Americans over sixty-five experience the pain of hemorrhoids. Hemorrhoids, which are swollen veins around the rectum and anus, may cause discomfort like itching, hurting, and even bleeding. They occur when these veins become irritated and enlarged from the pressure of bowel movements. Suggestions to help your parent prevent hemorrhoids or relieve symptoms include the following:

- Talk to your parent about constipation and suggest ways to avoid this.

- Make sure your parent has adequate fiber in his diet from whole grain bread, cereal products, raw fruits, and vegetables. Remember, 20 to 35 grams of fiber per day is recommended by the American Dietetic Association.

Of course, any change in bowel habits that include pain or bleeding should be reported to a physician. Symptoms of hemorrhoids may also indicate other medical problems.

Food and Drug Interactions. Mature adults take more medication than any other group of people in the United States today. The changing health of mature adults requiring daily medication places this age group at a higher risk for adverse reactions of some foods and drugs. The consequences of food-drug reaction range from constipation to vitamin or mineral deficiency. Reactions including a poor or uncontrollable appetite are also common.

Being aware of possible drug-nutrient interactions and food-drug interactions that can occur in your parent's drug regimen can help prevent or minimize the adverse effects of medications. Food can influence the absorption of medication, so it is wise to know how a medication should be taken. The state of your parent's stomach can decrease, delay, or increase the absorption of any medication.

Be sure to contact your parent's physician if you have any questions regarding medications and possible nutrient reactions, and follow the pharmacists instructions on each prescription and over-the-counter drug she takes.[1]

---

1. Harris H. McIlwain, et al., *The 50+ Wellness Program,* 135.

TAKE THE NUTRITION CHALLENGE

Beyond the problems mentioned in this chapter, your parent may have specific health problems such as high blood pressure, diabetes, cardiovascular disease, cancer, or others that require specific nutritional changes in the daily diet. It is vital that you and your parent meet with the doctor or a registered dietitian to discuss these specific problems and seek answers on how a special diet can enable your parent to be healthier and more energetic.

As you help your parent to plan a weekly menu, suggest low fat, high complex carbohydrate choices. Make sure there is plenty of fiber in the diet to avoid such problems as diverticulosis. And, most important, make sure the refrigerator and pantry are always filled with healthful, nutritious foods.

Eating to live instead of living to eat must become the key phrase for you and your parent. Depending on your parent's specific health problems, changing the daily diet may be a simple task or it could involve some drastic lifestyle changes—changes only your parent can make. But the rewards of being able to lead an active, normal life in the senior years are well worth any changes that must be made.

9

SOOTHING THE STRESSES OF AGING

"My mother has become so fearful," Bob reported over the phone. "Since she was diagnosed with diabetes several months ago, Mom has stayed in her home with the blinds drawn. When I go to visit she rarely has anything positive to say, talking only about these fears she has of growing old and dying."

Bob continued, "This behavior is so unlike her. Before this diagnosis, I could never find her at home. She was either playing golf with her friends, leading a woman's Bible study at church, or volunteering one day a week at the hospital. She used to have a smile on her face always, but not any more. What happened to the mom I once knew?"

For most of us, young and old, a diagnosis of a chronic disease can create stress and worry. All of a sudden we are faced with the reality of leaving our youth and growing older, which creates anxiety and fears. Some adults worry about the changes that can occur with aging, such as appearances, serious illnesses, loss of abilities, loneliness, and death. Many adults begin to confuse some of the normal changes in their bodies with changes caused by terminal diseases and fear these changes will result in complete immobility. Some may become so fearful that they sit at home and cease activity as they grow older. Worries about eating the right foods to prevent diseases or about normal changes in senses, such as hearing or seeing, begin to add to other health anxieties. Financial concerns may cause anxiety about living on a limited income.

The good news is that these are all normal and common fears; most people have these as they age. Many younger and middle-age adults have similar fears too! But most of these fears can be greatly eliminated when the facts are known. Throughout this book we have presented the most common facts about aging and have given you many practical strategies for assisting your parent. But for many adults, lack of knowledge about aging can cause much unnecessary stress and worry, which may lead to physical conditions such as hypertension. It does not have to be this way!

As we stated earlier, studies show that unresolved stress accounts for up to 80 percent of all diseases. Imagine how our lives would be if we could conquer this enemy of our mind. One research study set out to demonstrate how powerful an influence mental interpretation can be. A group of seventy-five-year-olds were placed in a retreat center for one week and told to be "fifty-five again." The center was equipped with surroundings (telephones, magazines) from twenty years prior. After one week this group of aging adults was tested. Amazingly, their hearing, eyesight, dexterity, and appetites improved. Their mental ability improved, and believe it or not, they actually measured taller in height![1]

What did this prove? It gives an interesting example of how worry, fear, and stress are of the mind. Even though life changes are more numerous and more frequent in old age, your parent can learn to replace fearful thoughts with positive ones, which can lead to recovery and abundant living.

STRESS IS A UNIVERSAL PROBLEM

Everyone experiences stress at one time or another. In the later years, the experience of stress is greatly compounded by a new sense of loss. Retirement is one type of loss senior adults experience as they give up power, income, and control. A physical ail-

---

1. Ellen J. Langer, *Mindfulness* (Reading, Mass.: Addison-Wesley, 1990).

ment or sudden decline in health is another common loss as aging adults lose control of their independence or daily activities, including meeting with friends, going to church, or purchasing their own groceries. Perhaps the greatest loss aging adults notice is becoming aware of personal mortality. "It just hit me this week after attending the funerals of my two best friends that I could be next. I am going to die," seventy-one-year-old Warren said.

UNDERSTANDING THE SENSE OF LOSS

As you care for an aging parent, be aware of the many losses your parent may have, such as Warren's losing his two best friends in one week. Perhaps your parent may have moved from the family homestead into a smaller apartment. Your parent may have lost some mental or physical capacity due to illness. He may have lost siblings and close friends to death. Whatever the loss is, know that it is very emotional and real to him and creates undue worry and stress. This stress may show up in a wide variety of physical changes and emotional responses, and these symptoms vary greatly from one person to the next. Perhaps the most universal sign of stress is a feeling of being pressured or overwhelmed.

RECOGNIZE WARNING SIGNS

Stress symptoms may vary from one person to the next, but in addition to feeling pressured or overwhelmed, senior adults may have these symptoms:

- Physical complaints: They may complain of stomach aches, headaches, diarrhea.

- Problems getting along with others: A congenial parent becomes obstinate.

- Behavior changes: The parent who was once in control has temper outbursts, unexplained anger, or cries for no reason.

- Regression: The parent begins to have behavior that is not age-appropriate.

- Sleep patterns: The parent starts to have nightmares or too little or too much sleep.

- Communication difficulty: Your parent's personality changes, such as a withdrawn person who suddenly requires much
attention or an extrovert who becomes withdrawn.

- Impatience: Your once considerate parent begins to have a
short circuit in behavior.

If your parent is experiencing a few of these characteristics,
chances are good that her level of stress, fear, or worry is excessive.
If left untreated, this stress can lead to permanent feelings of helplessness and ineffectiveness.

Not all stress is bad, however. In the United States today, there
are only about three one-hundred-year-olds per one hundred
thousand people. In some other societies studied there are as
many as forty to sixty per one hundred thousand. Close examination of such diverse societies shows one common link: The elderly
all have stress. In these other societies, the centenarians play an active part in the business of their community, both physically and
mentally, until the day they die.[2] Perhaps if we had no stress, we
might fade away. Some stress keeps us functioning, vital, and useful as we participate fully in our environment.

As we assist our aging parents in handling overwhelming stress,
we must help them learn to take control of their life instead of letting their life take control of them.

IDENTIFY AND REMOVE THE STRESS

The main strategy in dealing with stress is to identify and remove or reduce the source. Identification may be relatively easy,
but elimination could be a challenge, especially when the source
is a chronic illness, a terminally ill spouse, or financial problems
due to poor retirement planning. So it is important to find ways to
reduce the level of stress.

Many of us at any age suffer the side effects of chronic stress—
unresolved muscle tension, elevated blood pressure, increased
heartbeat, and general arousal—because we cannot get out of
"passing gear" (as opposed to normal or gearing down). Eventually the tension, arousal, and tightness seem normal, and we find
ourselves more vulnerable to illness and poor self-care habits.

---

2. Peter G. Hanson, *The Joy of Stress* (New York: Andrews, McMeel & Parker, 1985),
2.

Chronic tension can lead to knotted muscles, lower mobility, degenerative joint and spine problems, and exhaustion.

There are many ways to relax to overcome the effects of stress. We have found the relaxation response an important tool.

PRACTICE THE RELAXATION RESPONSE

Achieving relaxation through the relaxation response is important in helping your aging parent reduce some of the emotional stress of daily living. It can also be very useful for you, the caregiver, as you try to precariously balance the many demands in your life of work, family, and caring for an aging parent.

The relaxation response is a particular response of the body which can be very helpful. As we discussed previously, the loss that accompanies aging or living in fear of the unknown is a major source of stress, both physically and mentally. Research has shown that the relaxation response, used daily, can reduce stress, anxiety, tension, and pain. This relaxation develops an inner quiet and peacefulness, a calming of negative thoughts and worries, and a mental focus away from the source of stress.

STRESS AFFECTS CAREGIVER AND THE ELDERLY

The stress of caregiving or the stress of coping with loss puts an overload of emotional and mental demands on a person.

Growing older can often affect one's mood and causes irritability, impatience, and higher levels of frustration. The demands of caregiving can also affect one's mood, as you may already know!

While aging is thought of as a physical problem, the emotional fears and factors can play an overall role in the experience. Fear of aging or dying and the unknown life changes that accompany growing older can cause an increase in heart rate which stresses the heart.

RELAXATION CAN BE LEARNED

Relaxation can reduce physical strain and the emotional and negative thoughts; it can also increase your ability to self-manage stress and your parent's ability to cope with loss and worries.

Achieving relaxation uses a mental approach to activity in general rather than any one specific activity. For each of us, many different activities or routines may be relaxing, depending on our particular mental attitude. And what may be relaxing for one person can be frustrating or tension-producing for another. For example, some of us may find it calming and soothing to lie quietly and listen to a certain type of music; others may gain more relaxation from reading an enjoyable book. Remember that true relaxation involves more than just being still. You may not be relaxed just sitting in front of the TV. Some even have a high level of tension in their bodies and minds during sleep. An example would be those who toss and turn at night or who grind their teeth while asleep.

Relaxation is a skill that all people have the potential to develop. Some of us are naturally better at relaxing than others, but we can all learn to relax effectively. Much like learning to play the piano or tennis, becoming good at relaxation involves time, patience, and practice. Learning to relax deeply and effectively is a skill that develops gradually and cannot be rushed or hurried.

JUST TWENTY MINUTES A DAY

To begin your own relaxation program, you might try following these steps. Teach these steps to your parent or better still, try them together until everyone feels comfortable relaxing. During some part of your day, set aside a period of about twenty minutes for relaxation practice. This can be in the morning, afternoon, or evening; just pick a time when you may have few obligations or commitments so you will not feel hurried or rushed.

As much as possible, remove outside distractions that can disrupt your concentration: Turn off the radio, the television, even the ringer on the telephone, if need be. During practice, either lie flat or recline comfortably so that your whole body is supported, relieving as much tension or tightness in your muscles as you can. This is difficult to do upright, since your muscles must be tightened to maintain the position. You can use a pillow or cushion under your head, if this helps.

During the twenty-minute period, remain as still as possible; try to direct your thoughts away from the events of the day. Try to focus your thoughts as much as possible on the immediate moment, and eliminate any outside thoughts that may compete for your attention. Try to focus entirely on yourself and the different kinds of feelings or sensations you may notice throughout your body.

Try to notice which parts of your body feel relaxed and loose and which parts feel tense and uptight.

Picture Your Body at Peace

As you go through these steps, in your own way try to imagine that every muscle in your body is now becoming loose, relaxed, and free of any excess tension. Picture all of the muscles in your body unwinding; imagine them beginning to go loose and limp.

As you do this, concentrate on making your breathing nice and even, breathing slowly and in a regular fashion. With each exhaled breath, picture your muscles becoming even more relaxed, as if with each breath you somehow breathe the tension away. At the end of twenty minutes, take a few moments to examine the feelings and sensations you have been able to achieve. Notice whether areas that felt tight and tense at first now feel more loose and relaxed, and whether any areas of tension or tightness remain.

Do not be surprised if the relaxed feeling you achieve begins to fade and dissipate once you get up and return to your normal activities. Many people find that it is only after several weeks of daily, consistent practice that they are able to maintain the relaxed feeling beyond the practice session itself.[3]

If it seems hard to relax or if you feel your parent needs to learn about an individual approach for relaxation and stress management, you might see a clinical psychologist who specializes in these problems. Whether you use the techniques we have discussed or choose formal training by a professional, learning to relax effectively can help control the stresses of caregiving and the emotions of aging. It can increase positive thinking and lessen the impact of this stress on one's overall lifestyle.

Getting Back in Control of Your Life

As your parent ages, you will find that some things just cannot be changed. Terminal illnesses can happen, and your parent will change physically and mentally. A parent may no longer recognize you or the grandchildren, and they will die.

---

3. Harris H. McIlwain, et al., *Winning with Chronic Pain* (New York: Prometheus Books, 1994), 142.

But the way we all, parents and adult children, react to these changes, will affect every avenue of life. Have you ever known someone who experienced a great deal of tragedy and suffering, yet she kept on going and actively caring for those around them? Shirley, age eighty-four, is like that. Just seven months after her husband died of a heart attack at age sixty-seven, her only son, Pete, was killed in a diving accident. Shirley handled that unbelievably well; then less than a year later she found out that she had breast cancer. She had already lost a mother and sister to this type of cancer, but at age sixty-four, Shirley was determined to beat this. All of this occurred twenty years ago, and Shirley is still as active as ever in the church and community. You see, she is a survivor and has leaned on her strong faith in God and network of friends for support. People like Shirley who are survivors take the annoying interruptions that occur as their special challenges in life and lean on faith for their strength.

We have given you some of the most common negative areas you might experience with aging parents. By understanding their stresses and feelings of loss, you can help them develop very effective strategies for coping and for better enjoyment of life.

HANDLING DENIAL

Ideally we all should begin to prepare for our senior years while we are still young, realizing that each day we grow older. Aging parents have to accept the reality of aging along with its limitations and be ready to make modifications in their lives.

Denial or nonacceptance is often the way aging parents try to preserve self-esteem. They may feel that if they admit they need help at home or need financial assistance with groceries, rent, or prescriptions, friends and family will think less of them. This is certainly not the case. Acceptance of all aspects of aging is the first step in successful communication.

Here are some steps to help your parent reach acceptance.

- Ask your parent to keep a daily journal and list her activities, feelings, and any concerns. Tell her this will help you know how to help. Look at this journal together at the end of a week and the end of the month. Talk about problem areas, and let your parent know that you love her no matter what happens. Assure your parent that you can assist when necessary.

- Talk about your own aging. Look through photo albums from when you were a child. Find pictures of your parents at your age and your grandparents when they were elderly. Talk about the changes in everyone through the years, and affirm the love and respect you have for older relatives.

- Encourage your parent to talk with his physician about complaints or bodily changes that are new. Let him know that many people are going through the same situation, and the best attitude is a positive one.

- Get your parent to join the AARP or other senior organizations (see list of resources and organizations in chap. 10). Find activities "just for seniors" in your community, and take your parent to meet others of the same age. Having a supportive family is important, but it is also necessary for seniors to have a circle of caring friends who are undergoing the same transitions.

- Intervention can often help if you still find that your parent is denying increasing age and limitations. You may find that your pastor can talk about life stages, or another family member can bring this out in the open. How your parent accepts this stage in his life determines when positive coping skills can be implemented.

Dealing with Anxiety and Fears

Many elderly adults have a surplus of fears, some very real and others only imagined. Some common fears older adults question include:

- What if my spouse dies and I have to live alone?

- What if my children ignore me or quit taking care of me?

- What if my spouse leaves me and I have no money or home?

- Will I have this nagging pain until the day I die?

- What if I am walking outside and I fall when there is no one to help me?

- What if I am robbed or beaten up during the night by a burglar and my children are out of town?

- What if something happens and I run out of money?

- What if Medicare does not pay for my hospitalization or nursing home?

- What if the bank takes over my home? Where will I live?

- What if no one comes to see me anymore or calls me?

- What if I cannot afford medicine or food?

- What if I can no longer take care of myself?

- What if my children think I am a burden?

- What if I have to stop going to church due to illness or because I have no transportation?

If an aging parent is obsessive about fears, he will be unable to move beyond them. We have found that it is best to talk openly about the fears and seek ways to change the negative thinking. Worrying about future disaster or impending illness helps no one, but changing these worries with positive thoughts will enable your parent to think clearly and productively.

You can help your parent reduce anxiety and fear.

- Ask your parent to write down the situations that cause anxiety and fear—a certain program or newscast on television, a family member who is not patient, conflict with a neighbor, a friend who is always depressed, even reading the morning paper. If the fears are reasonable, encourage your parent to avoid these situations when possible so as not to be confronted with these areas.

- Do not try to talk your parent out of obsessive fears if she is too agitated. Find a licensed mental health counselor and make an appointment to "talk it out" with an impartial trained professional who understands these problems. Medication may be necessary to help reduce the anxiety that accompanies stress in aging.

- Teach your parent how to do the relaxation response. Do this with him a few times, and put a calendar on the refrigerator to check off as he tries to relax. Tell him about the benefits you experience from the relaxation response. To be beneficial, your parent should do this at least twice a day.

- Some researchers have found it helpful to replace fears and worries with positive thoughts of the moment. For example, instead of dwelling on a past conflict with a friend or family member, encourage your parent to think only of an event that is occurring at the moment, such as baking that pie or going shopping or visiting with a grandchild. Every time the fear or worry comes to mind, immediately replace it with a positive thought. Remember no one else can eliminate your parent's nagging fears. He or she must take control of these thoughts and replace them with positive thinking.

- Get your parent to join a Bible study group or fellowship group. Most churches have ongoing activities for members. If there is no senior program in the neighborhood, meet with the pastor and offer your support in starting one. The Scriptures offer hope and assurance for all when fears and worries intrude in one's life.

SUSPICIONS TOWARD OTHERS

As your parent ages and experiences loss or illness, he may be more sensitive to the thoughts and actions of others. Constant, unrelenting fears accompanying this life stage can often result in distorted thoughts and behavior. This does not mean that your parent is crazy! Instead, it means that the stress has affected the interpretation of what people do and say.

If you find that your parent seems overly suspicious, talk about this behavior. Sometimes the fear of the unknown is often stressful enough to distort one's thinking. Here are some ways to help your parent cope with suspicion.

- Get your parent to trust you as he tells you his suspicions. This involves not taking these lightly but listening with empathy.

- Have your parent write down the suspicions when these occur and the feelings they bring on (panic, increased heart rate, trembling, nausea, diarrhea). Go over these together and talk about people who arouse suspicions. Is there an alternative explanation for his actions?

- If the suspicions seem reasonable, go with your parent to confront the person involved. Sometimes facing up to the suspicion and hearing the other person's response will help alleviate the fear in your parent's mind.

- Once the suspicion has been resolved, be firm with your parent about controlling his mind. Remember that harboring negative thoughts about others is detrimental to one's health and general outlook on life.

ANGER AND IRRITABILITY

Anger is a typical reaction to many changes that accompany aging, but how one reacts to the anger can vary from one person to another. When an aging parent allows anger to consume her whole being, intervention is necessary.

To help your parent cope with the anger and irritability that often accompanies aging, the feelings should first be understood. Then the energy spent on being angry can be replaced with positive actions to make the best of golden years.

Upfront anger is expressed directly toward the person or situation at which the person is angry. This type of anger, if not overemphasized, is most acceptable as the person expresses feelings to the one involved. Statements such as "Yes, that doctor bill made me mad" or "I get so angry when your father leaves his clothes around" are acceptable *if* your parent does not follow through with violent outbursts.

Displaced anger originates from strong feelings toward a person or event but is directed toward a different person or event. For example, your mother may fuss at your father one day and suggest that "maybe he needs to get out of the chair and move around." Instead of expressing his anger toward her for the comment, your father calls you on the phone and yells at you, expressing *displaced anger*. This is painful anger as the parent loses control and lets off steam by spewing harsh words on innocent victims.

Inward anger is unexpressed, either verbally or nonverbally. Instead of speaking openly about angry thoughts, your parent may let it boil up inside, resulting in physical ailments such as nausea, tension headaches, muscle aches, or even depression.

You will need to help a parent cope with anger and irritability.

- You must talk with your parent about the dangers of anger that is not expressed in a positive manner. Anger can destroy health as well as relationships with loved ones.

- Ask your parent to write down the very situations or people who cause anger—the newspaper that is found in the bushes each morning, a neighbor who lets her dog bark all hours of the night, grandchildren who rarely come to visit, even you for not giving her enough attention. Try to arrive at a solution to each problem such as contacting the newspaper about the problem, a polite phone call to the neighbor, or encouraging your children to be more attentive.

- Let your parent know that anger is an acceptable emotion, but it must be expressed in a way that will not injure her health or people around her.

- If your parent seems unable to control anger, seek the help of a pastor or physician. Ask for a recommendation of a professional who can offer help for coping with anger.

LOSING CONTROL

In addition to feelings of anger and irritability, an aging parent may feel the loss of control over many aspects of her life. Where she was once the head of the clan, she is now the pampered guest at family gatherings. A parent who was CEO for a major corporation before retirement and now lives with the unending pain of arthritis each day may feel he is of no worth. Instead of controlling his destiny as he did in younger years, many elderly adults may now feel as if growing old controls every aspect of his being—day in and day out.

What are the elderly afraid of losing? The list is long and includes their spouse, your help, independence, self-esteem, privacy, grandchildren's respect, ability to participate fully in life to financial security, mental stability, and memory. With your help your parent can cope with the loss of control in the following ways.

- If your parent does become distraught because of loss of control, talk about these feelings and fears. Again, remind him of the list he made and help him learn to channel these feelings into another direction that he does have control over.

- Some areas your parent will lose control over, such as cooking meals or driving to the grocery store. Find help for him in these areas. It is not a sign of personal failure to get assistance from anyone—we all need help at sometime in our lives.

- Help your parent make a list of areas he has lost control—a certain activity, sleep habits, freedom to spend money, ability to see friends regularly. Also list the areas he still has control over—cooking, walking outdoors each morning, playing with grandchildren, attending Sunday School, taking care of a garden or plants. With the help of the physician, pastor, family, and friends, encourage your parent to concentrate on those areas in life where there is still control.

- Encourage your parent to set goals each day to tackle a new area where he has lost control. Perhaps he could start an exercise program at a senior center to help with walking. Maybe she could help a grandchild cook a meal, getting help with reaching and bending over. Your parent can approach other areas in his life the same as this—one step at a time—until he begins to live the life he deserves. Remember, taking one small step at a time, then another, and another, will let your parent regain control and confidence over those areas in life that have been shut out.

BECOMING SOCIALLY ISOLATED

Social isolation may be a three-faceted problem for your aging parent. First, they may purposefully avoid some friends and family members due to fatigue or irritability. She prefers to stay secluded in the home with doors locked and shades drawn.

Second, friends and family members may be purposely avoiding him. "Gramps is always complaining," one college-age young man said. "I get tired of hearing him lecture me so I quit visiting."

Perhaps your parent has driven friends away because of constant complaining. "I'm so sorry," one elderly woman said. "I cannot visit my sister anymore because she constantly cries about her declining health. I'm not so active anymore either, but dwelling on it does not help anyone."

Third, for some aging parents, leaving the bed or house can be associated with wellness. They may be fearful that some people who see them "out and about" may assume they are back to "normal." Once they are considered better, family and friends may be quick to expect them to do things they are afraid of doing.

Social isolation is a problem that will take time to correct. Here are some ways to cope with the situation:

- Encourage your parent to live each day fully. You may arrange for transportation to senior activities, an adult day care, or church functions.

- When your parent begins "me-related" conversations, try to stop this behavior before she gets caught up in obsessive worries. Change the subject, go to another part of the house, or take a drive to focus on something other than self.

- Continue to affirm that friends are the best support system anyone can have, and make plans to entertain his friends at home. You may invite friends over to visit and prepare a light lunch or take your parent over to friends' homes.

- Encourage your parent to go on at least one outing each week and more, if she is able. Go to the zoo, an amusement park, a museum, or to the beach for an evening stroll. Take pictures and keep a journal recording the events, sights, and experiences you have. When your parent begins having self-doubts, show him the journal and talk about the good feelings he has when he is with friends and going places.

SELF-CENTEREDNESS

When an aging parent goes into the hospital for surgery or diagnostic testing, family members focus on helping until the patient is up and about again. However, when your parent has health problems that go on for months or years, there is a tendency for your parent to expect everyone's life to revolve around his. It is difficult to change this pattern once it becomes routine.

Aging parents may let you know "My problems are worse than anyone I know" or "You will never know how horrible I feel." While your parent probably does not intend to be a burden on anyone, he may have fallen into a pattern of focusing solely on self. This is easy to do when all thoughts and actions have revolved around her for a period of time.

Think about it. When an aging parent becomes ill, all the children and grandchildren rush home. The parent is pampered and waited on by nurses and doctors in the hospital, receiving all sorts of affirming attention. Neighbors bring meals, the pastor makes a call, extended family members send flowers and cards, and church members add him to the prayer chain. Who would ever want to be well after getting all this attention!

But if this routine has occurred in your home, do not place blame on either side. Instead, talk with your parent and begin to initiate changes that are more other-centered than self-centered.

- Ask your parent to set aside thirty minutes each day to focus on problems. During the thirty minutes she is to think only of herself, no one else. But the rest of the time each day she is to focus on anything except herself. She can wear a rubber band on her wrist as a reminder that if she begins to worry during the "off" time. If she can follow this routine, she may find that her worry time lessens and thoughts about others become more frequent.

- Let your siblings and family members know that the parent is self-absorbed. Encourage them to change the subject when the parent begins talking about how unfortunate he is or how horrible her surgery was. If the parent is now well or on the road to recovery, changing the subject will let her know that you love her but want her to be more positive about life.

- Let your parent know that self-absorption is not acceptable in social situations. When at church or group meetings, encourage him to talk more about others and less about his own problems.

- If your parent continues to be absorbed in his own needs all the time, seek help with a mental health counselor.

Abuse to Loved Ones

Many aging parents know that family is most important to their well-being, but they still treat you worse than outsiders. One middle-age daughter of aging parents said, "My parents can be so happy around their siblings or personal friends. Then when I call the next day, they criticize the way I raise my children or tell me my husband is not a good provider. I don't get it."

Perhaps when you were younger your parent did criticize you as a means of discipline. But now that you are an adult, this method is no longer acceptable. Your parent must quit the abuse, with your help. Consider these guidelines:

- Communication is vital in this situation as you let a parent know that while you are still her son or daughter, you are now an adult and will not listen to verbal abuse.

- Encourage your parent to get in the habit of treating you and other family members as guests. Remember, when the chips are down, the family members are the ones who will be there. Do not let anger drive you away.

- Monitor your parent's angry responses toward you and others, and talk about redirecting this anger.

- Walk away when a parent begins verbal abuse. Announce, "I won't be treated this way. You are out of control. I'll come back in a little while (or another day) when you can treat me with love and respect."

- When harsh words are said, apologies are greatly appreciated. If friends or other family members have been abused verbally, encourage your parent to call and say "I'm sorry."

Stress

"Stressed out" is a term used to describe the impact that life stressors have on all of us. Stress can cause anxiety, tension, high blood pressure, depression, and anger—all detrimental to your parent's health. Your parent may now experience many stressors, including physical stressors (a chronic or terminal disease, the pain of arthritis, an inability to remember), social stressors (the loss of spouse, close friends and siblings, the loss of activities), work stressors (retirement), and family stressors (feeling of dependency on others, family members who do not visit as much).

Your aging parent does have every right to be stressed, but certain actions can be taken to cope with stress.

1. Have your parent write down the things that make them "stressed," including health problems, finances, the fear of living in a nursing home, living with a spouse who has senility, and more. Have him make a conscious effort to put aside the things he cannot control and focus on the positive aspect of life—a new grandbaby, a cruise next summer, going to the church social, a granddaughter's graduation from college, a flower garden.

2. If your parent is experiencing any physical symptoms of stress—such as high blood pressure, headaches, palpitations or anxiety attacks—be sure to consult the physician.

3. Take your parent to a class on stress management offered through your community center or wellness programs.

4. A therapist who specializes in stress management could help your parents learn ways of dealing with overwhelming problems, people, and situations.

5. Relaxation tapes are available at local book stores or learn how to do the relaxation response outlined in this chapter. Do the tapes or relaxation response with your parents until they grasp the importance of this time-out.

MILD DEPRESSION

While major (clinical) depression is less prevalent among the elderly than in younger groups, many older people commonly experience situational or chronic symptoms of mild depression.

Perhaps your parent tells you she doesn't feel depressed, and outwardly she may seem happy. But she may still be experiencing mild depression. Depressive symptoms can include these:

- disturbances in sleep patterns

- loss of interest in usual activities

- weight loss or gain (more than 5 percent of body weight)

- fatigue

- impaired thinking

- thoughts of dying or suicide

- depressed thoughts or irritability

- mood swings

- staying at home all the time

- avoidance of special friends

- difficulty concentrating

- feelings of worthlessness or excessive or inappropriate guilt

- agitation or, in contrast, a general slowing of intentional bodily activity

Nathan S. Kline wrote in *From Sad to Glad* an interesting perspective on depression, saying depression might be defined as the magnified and inappropriate expression of some otherwise quite common emotional responses. That, of course, is true of many other disorders. By way of analogy, one expects to find heart palpitation in a person who has just run up a steep hill.

Something is decidedly amiss, however, if such palpitation occurs during a sedate walk. So, too, with depression. All of us experience moments of sadness, loneliness, pessimism, and uncertainty as a natural reaction to particular circumstances.

In the depressed person these feelings become all-pervasive; they can be triggered by the least incident or occur without evident connection to any outside cause. At times there may be a sudden burst of tears that the person cannot explain—or more or less constant weepiness.[4]

Depression is debilitating. As many as 12 to 14 million Americans are affected with it each year. This figure extends to as many as 13 to 20 percent of the total population in the United States having depression at any given time. And most researchers find that twice as many women succumb to depression as men.

Depression generally occurs when negative thoughts get so rooted into the subconscious that the person cannot break out of the cycle of negativism and self-pity. If left untreated, depression can last for months or even years, leading to feelings of helplessness and, at worst, suicide. It is not a sign of personal weakness or

---

4. Nathan S. Kline, *From Sad to Glad* (New York: Ballentine, 1974), 6–7.

moral corruption. People can no more pull themselves together and get over depression than they can will away diabetes.

Depression comes in several forms, from a major depressive episode to a chronic, low-grade depression called *dysthymia*. Dysthymia is defined as being in a depressed mood more days than not for at least two years.[5]

Depression is a very complicated affliction, and not as easy to deal with as other worries and stressors mentioned in this chapter. Many times depression can be rooted within a person, stemming from a biochemical imbalance or a symptom of an underlying ailment. And quite often professional medical help is needed to maintain, control, and cure depression with medication and therapy. Many excellent prescription drugs and many medical protocols can assist greatly if this is the case.

If your parent has the symptoms listed for depression on a regular basis, you should seek professional help for them. Follow the physician's advice in taking medication and/or receiving therapy to alleviate the problem.

- See a qualified mental health specialist if depression immobilizes your parent. Studies show that up to 85 percent of patients will find relief through treatment with antidepressant medications, psychotherapy, or electroshock therapy.

- If your parent has suicidal thoughts, take these seriously. Again, seek professional help.

- Alcohol and drugs cannot combat depression. Make certain that your parent only uses medication prescribed by the physician.

- Exercise is a great cure for easing mild depression. Determine what your parent can do physically and start a program. Talk with the doctor about such a program as one way to help lessen her sadness. Physical activities can increase mental alertness for elderly adults.

- Depressed individuals must stick to a routine each day. Staying in bed all day, unless advised by a doctor, will not help alleviate depressive feelings.

---

5. "Bluer Than Blue," *Involved*, St. Vincent's Health System (Fall 1993), 2.

- Reaching out to others is a great way to get out of depression. It greatly reduces actions such as brooding, moping, or too much self- introspection.

- Encourage your parent to find some humor, joy, and pleasure at least once a day. Try the newspaper cartoons, or even the situation comedies on TV. Your parent should try to have at least one good laugh a day to combat sadness. Often, body functions decrease before the mind. When this happens, mental stimulation should increase or at least be maintained.

- The local church has endless activities for people to get involved in, whether for personal nurture or volunteering. Encourage your parent to become active in a weekly Bible study and to offer one morning a week to visit shut-ins or help in the church office. Social intervention increases sensory awareness, cognitive functioning, and preserves social skills for the aged.

Death

It is never easy to accept death. Even with the hope Christians have of life eternal, losing a loved one causes feelings of anger, confusion, and sadness. Your parent may not know how to express these feelings of loss when a spouse or close friend dies. But you must encourage her to work through these feelings because they are inevitable. Accepting and realizing the emotional loss that we all will temporarily face is one big step on the road to dealing with death.

Help your parents cope with the reality of death in the following ways:

- Probably the best way to assist an aging parent in coping with death is to face the reality beforehand. Accept that death is going to happen to all of us. Acknowledge that Christian loved ones will one day be leaving this life for eternal life with Jesus Christ. Therefore, we must urge our parent to live today so as not to have regrets when the event comes.

- In order to avoid feelings of guilt later, talk about expressing love and kindness to a spouse, family members, and friends. In other words, your parent should have no regrets and guilt when loved ones pass away. Ask, "What if Mom (or Dad or a loved one) were to die today? What should you have told them? What regrets might you have if you don't?"

- Remind your parent to not let life revolve around just one person, even if it is a spouse. Although that might sound a bit insensitive, there is danger when many elderly couples have lived their lives isolated together. They have cultivated no outside friends, activities, or interests. While this may sound beautiful and romantic, it is not realistic to the remaining spouse when the other dies.

Urge your parent to develop a full life now including outside interests, friends, clubs, and social activities. While not hurting the marital relationship, her horizons will be expanded. Having a "circle of friends" permits each parent to continue living once the spouse dies.

- After the death of a spouse, help your parent get on with life. Again, this requires a realistic and wholesome outlook, and some anticipation that this time will come. If the parent is realistic, he or she will grieve for a period of time but should not allow mourning to become obsessive. Consider professional counseling if you find your parent is not responding to the world each day and living in grief or in the past.[6]

The Importance of Funerals. Funerals are a positive force in the grieving process and can be helpful to everyone. As stated earlier, death is not easy to face or to accept for anyone, but funerals can help us to work through our feelings. A funeral is a ritual that can help focus emotions and bring meaning to the experience of death. The funeral serves as a means to commemorate the deceased, but just as importantly, it helps the survivors to heal emotionally. When a spouse or close friend dies, your parent will experience the horrible pain of grief, and even though it hurts, grief is not something to avoid. This part of the healing process allows us to separate ourselves from the deceased person and to move forward with our lives.

Funerals give Christians permission to express their feelings of sadness and loss. They also stimulate persons to begin talking about the deceased, one of the first steps toward accepting death. In fact, people who do not attend the funeral of a loved

---

6. Harris H. McIlwain, et al., *50+ Wellness Program,* 247.

one because they want to deny the death may suffer from unresolved grief several months later. To resolve this grief, people
need to accept the reality of death not only on an intellectual level but on an emotional level as well. It is for this reason that many
funerals in our culture are usually preceded by an open-casket
visitation period. Research has found that the viewing of the deceased person helps you to accept the death of that person, and
this helps with grieving because it shows that there is no return
to this life. Funeral directors and clergy persons are helpful in
guiding persons through this time, but, again, the real key to
coping with this time is preplanning and talking about the even-
tuality of death.

With death comes life. The time of the death of a loved one can
also be a time of opportunity for the remaining spouse. Sometimes the spouse has had the burden of care and the responsibility
for the person. With that person's death, the surviving spouse is
often freed up for new dimensions of living and new opportunities
never explored before.

Sometimes the windfalls of judicious planning, such as life insurance policies, also provide an economic stability and freedom
that allows greater flexibility in life. Often the burden of many
years of constantly caring for an invalid or terminally ill spouse can
become unbearable. Opportunities can now be taken for the living parent to enrich his own life. Be aware of these needs in your
practical planning for your parent during time of loss.

Death is an unavoidable reality, but with faith, proper living,
and planning—and a devout belief in Jesus Christ as our personal saviour—it need not be a crippling experience. With the proper outlook, death is a life change that surviving spouses can
survive.

Death is temporary. One of the most meaningful funerals we attended was of a dynamic Christian woman who lived life to the fullest. Even though her death was untimely, she had planned her
funeral to be a celebration of life and love for family and friends.
The following prose, written by the Carmelite Monastery, Tallow
County, Waterford, Ireland, was printed in the bulletin for her funeral. Perhaps this says exactly what death to a Christian should be
. . . a moment of separation, but we will all soon be united together
with God.

Togetherness

. . . I have only slipped away into the next room.
Whatever we were to each other, that we are still.
Call me by my old familiar name,
speak to me in the easy way which you always used.
Laugh as we always laughed together.
Play, smile, think of me, pray for me.
Let my name be the household word it always was.
Let it be spoken without effort.
Life means all that it ever meant.
It was the same as it ever was;
there is absolutely unbroken continuity.
Why should I be out of your mind
because I am out of your sight?
I am but waiting for you, for an interval,
somewhere very near just around the corner.
All is well.
Nothing is past; nothing is lost.
One brief moment and all will be as it was before—
only better, infinitely happier and forever,
we will all be one together with God.

YOU ARE NOT ALONE

Many studies now show what Christians have known for years, that there is a positive association between religious commitment and health in later life. One recent study performed by Duke University Medical Center studied the relationship between religion, aging, and health. This study indicated that one-quarter to one-third of older adults find religion the most important factor in coping with physical illness and other stresses.

People of faith who attended church frequently have lower blood pressure and fewer strokes; lower rates of depression, anxiety and alcoholism; higher life satisfaction and greater well-being; and better ability to adapt to the rigors of physical illness and disability. Furthermore, religious people perceive themselves as less disabled and experience less pain than do those with similar health problems but without a strong faith in God.[7]

---

7. Harold G. Koenig and Andrew J. Weaver, "Faith Eases Potential Aches and Pains of Aging," *The United Methodist Reporter* (July 29, 1994), 4.

Encourage your parent to stay involved in church no matter what trials he or she is going through emotionally. A strong faith in God can offer peace even when the latest therapies fail.

Your parent may experience these or other issues in everyday life, and some may seem insurmountable. As you read this chapter, circle those areas your parent needs to work on and help him get back in control with the helpful tips. As a caregiver, you must know that you are not alone! Millions of people your age are sandwiched between raising children, managing careers, and caring for aging parents. But the more assertive you are in finding answers, the sooner your parents can make healthful changes in thinking and actions. If the problems seem unsurmountable, know that trained professionals are ready to guide you and your parent in a positive direction. Ask for help.

10

FINANCING
LONG-TERM CARE

Americans are living longer, and that is good news! But due to a longer lifespan, many elderly adults are faced with unplanned financial responsibilities that can end in disaster, such as paying for emergency home care due to a disability or illness, the skyrocketing cost of long-term care in nursing homes, and the cost of unexpected surgery or an extended hospital stay. The cost of nursing home care for Alzheimer's disease alone may be approximately $40,000 a year, with the total cost for this disease from diagnosis to death exceeding $210,000. These concerns not only affect aging parents, but they will have a tremendous impact on the adult child trying to balance finances and the ensuing emotions when crisis occurs.

In the best situations, financial planning should be an ongoing process throughout a lifetime. Yet you may find that your parent has to exist on a budget far less than the amount he had as a younger and middle-aged adult due to lack of planning in earlier years. The burden of having to pay unexpected medical bills, combined with increasing inflation and health care costs during the senior years, can ultimately take its toll on health and well-being, often resulting in anxiety, depression, and stress-related illnesses.

No matter how adequately (or inadequately) your parent planned for retirement, you can take some steps now to establish a more secure financial situation. Then, together, you can make the necessary changes to cover emergency expenses.

There is a cost to aging for Americans today, and planning for that cost is essential with adult children fully participating in the financial discussion. One couple, John and Sharon, talked with their parents openly about finances, medical expenses, living costs, and more. "It was very awkward at first," John told us, "because Sharon's parents are in such good health. We didn't want to mention a negative subject and bring everyone down. But so many of our friends' parents are having major health and financial problems that we wanted to prevent impending disaster if we could."

John and Sharon, like millions of other adult children, are very wise to begin planning for their parent's long-term care and senior years before a health or financial crisis occurs. This allows the parent to have input into the type of care he or she wants (should each become unable to live alone) and how this is to be paid for.

But for as many adult children who plan with their parents, millions more maintain a "wait and see" attitude hoping that "things will work out" should a parent have health problems. Heidi realized the hazards of this attitude. "I thought everything was wonderful with Mom and Dad. They were healthy, active in their church and community, and had a comfortable living. Then Dad had a stroke and had to be moved to a nursing home for round-the-clock medical care. Within one year, everything my parents owned was wiped out—all their retirement investments, their savings, any hope for a future. Dad died within a year of having the stroke, leaving Mom virtually poverty-stricken. It was the most devastating time in our lives."

WHO WILL PAY FOR LONG-TERM CARE?

Most adult children, like Heidi, do not consider the reality of long-term care for aging parents until it is too late, and they end up paying for this out of their own savings or losing all their life's investments. Some adult children have had to choose between paying for a parent's care or assisting their own child with college costs. But it does not have to be this way if you plan and try to foresee situations that could happen.

You can review the following coverage available through Social Security, trusts, investments, Medicare, Medigap, Medicaid, and long-term care insurance, and also look into any state or federally assisted care programs that might be available in your area.

TAKE TIME TO PLAN AHEAD

We believe that the senior years should not be devastating in any way—financially, emotionally, or physically—if you plan and prevent. As you begin laying out a financial plan for your parent, review the material in this chapter and contact those services that apply to your parent's needs and resources. If your parent has an estate with minimum assets, then check on those state or federally-funded services that are available at little or no cost. Adults with larger estates might need the services of professionals such as an attorney, insurance agent, financial planner, accountant (CPA), and more.

After you have done your homework, help your parent evaluate the various options and work out a plan for long-term care before this is needed. Fill in the suggested inventories given later in this chapter to get a total picture of assets and liabilities, establish a workable budget for your parent, and let the size of the estate dictate the direction of your planning.

SOCIAL SECURITY

Social Security is a federal government program available for all of us upon retirement, if we become severely disabled, or after death. It is designed to replace part of the income people normally would receive from employment. Before you consider any of the many options to long-term care, get started with financial planning by calling your parent's Social Security office and requesting the free brochures available for retirement planning. Upon qualifying, your parent will receive monthly benefits and insurance protection from Social Security. Your parent can receive these benefits as early as age sixty-two, with the amount depending on how old they are, when they apply, and the lifetime earnings on which they paid Social Security taxes (the higher their earnings, the higher the benefit rate will be). You can call toll-free at 1-800-772-1213 for information.

Approaches to Funding Long-Term Care

Many avenues exist to fund long-term care. The following are some of the most common types seniors use.

Trusts

For those who can afford it, trusts are ideal vehicles to planning for the future. Often these trusts allow assets to pass to the children when elderly parents are infirmed, thus taking the financial burden off the backs of the children.

With your parent, check into the trust department of a large, reputable bank and get details on placing his assets with him rather than handling these yourself. The benefits of a trustee are extensive, including immortality, objectivity, and freedom from personal bias, prompt execution of investment orders, experience in managing assets, familiarity with tax laws, and more. A CPA or accountant can guide your parent in establishing trusts and give you an idea of fees, services, and minimum account standards.

Investments

If your parent has investments but has not reviewed these with a financial advisor lately, make an appointment with a reputable planner. Get references from your parent's attorney, accountant, friends, or banker for a planner who understands the needs of the elderly and long-term care. The International Association for Financial Planning can also provide a list of members in your parent's hometown (1-800-945-4237).

The direction of your parent's investments should depend on the size of the assets to invest and how soon the cash might be needed. The planner might recommend federally insured CDs, short-term treasury bills, and money market accounts for those funds needed within five years. For a longer period of investment, the planner might consider placing some funds in conservative, no load, growth, and income mutual funds. At this point in your parent's life, avoid high risk, high return investments. Be sure to become educated before your meeting with a financial planner and seek additional advice from magazines such as *Money, Kiplinger, Personal Finance,* and others.

MEDICARE

Medicare is the basic health insurance program for people aged sixty-five or older and for many people with disabilities.

Medicare has two parts:

1. Hospital insurance (often called Part A). This helps pay for inpatient hospital care and certain follow-up services.

2. Medical insurance (sometimes called Part B). This helps pay for doctors' services, outpatient hospital care, and other medical services.

If your parent is sixty-five years old or over and is already receiving Social Security benefits, he or she will automatically be enrolled in Medicare, although there is the opportunity to turn down Part B. If a person is disabled, he will be automatically enrolled in Medicare after receiving disability benefits for twenty-four months; again, Part B can be turned down if desired. If your parent is sixty-five years old and wants to continue working but does not want Social Security, then he should call or visit a Social Security office to decide if he may want to sign up for Medicare only.

There are many other rules associated with Medicare enrollment, including some penalties for not enrolling in Part B when your parent is first eligible. Your Social Security office can give you more details.

Medicare hospital insurance (Part A) pays for the following:

- inpatient hospital care

- skilled nursing facility care

- home health care

- hospice care

Medicare medical insurance (Part B) pays for:

- doctors' services

- outpatient hospital services

- home health visits

- diagnostic x-ray, laboratory, and other tests

- necessary ambulance services

- other medical services and supplies

Medicare does not pay for:

- custodial care

- dentures and routine dental care

- eyeglasses, hearing aids, and examinations to prescribe and fit them

- nursing home care (except skilled nursing care)

- prescription drugs

- routine physical checkups and related tests

Health Maintenance Organizations (HMOs)

HMOs contracting with the Medicare program must provide the same coverage offered by fee-for-service Medicare plans, and Medicare pays the HMO on a monthly prepaid basis for each person enrolled. The same and often additional benefits are offered by these organizations.

Once your parent is enrolled in an HMO plan, he may be charged a monthly premium and copayment instead of the deductibles and coinsurance amounts paid by fee-for-service beneficiaries. In most cases, if your parent is an HMO enrollee, she does not need Medigap coverage because the plan may provide all or most of the benefits.

Many HMO plans have contracts with the Medicare program and also provide benefits beyond those Medicare pays for, such as preventive care, prescription drugs, dental care, hearing aids, and eyeglasses. The benefits vary from plan to plan, and you will need to find out the specific benefits offered by each.

An important note: When your parent enrolls in the HMO, he will only see the designated plan providers, except in case of an emergency. Should your parent become unhappy with the HMO, he can again enroll in regular Medicare. If he dropped his Medigap coverage on joining the HMO and wants to seek this coverage on leaving the HMO, he may have trouble covering preexisting conditions until the end of a waiting period. Help your parent consider the repercussions before dropping the Medigap policy.

SUPPLEMENTAL INSURANCE (MEDIGAP)

Medigap insurance can help pick up the amount that Medicare does not pay and limit the amount your parent must pay. In past years, the Medigap policies varied a great deal causing some confusion, until 1992 when Congress authorized ten fixed standardized plans. The insurance companies can only offer this type coverage, but some companies may not sell all ten policies. This makes it easier to compare coverage and premiums between insurers.

This coverage will usually fill any gaps in Medicare coverage (primarily deductibles and copayment). Some policies can include coverage for non-Medicare items such as prescription drugs, vision and hearing care, dental, home health care, and even routine exams. Coverage is also available for the difference between the doctors' bills and the Medicare-allowed charge when your parent's doctor does not take Medicare assignment. The cost will be in relation to the coverage chosen. Other policies like hospital indemnities, cancer coverage, and long-term care policies should not be considered adequate supplements to Medicare.

LONG-TERM CARE INSURANCE

Long-term care insurance is another vehicle used to pay for care in the senior years. Studies have shown that more than 40 percent of Americans who turn sixty-five this year will eventually enter a nursing home. For most, the stay will be measured in months, for others in years, and the cost of nursing home care can be staggering. While this type of protection is often costly, *long-term care insurance* allows the aging adult to keep a strong hold on his savings and investments.

Approximately 50 percent of the cost of long-term care is paid by individuals. One nonprofit organization, United Seniors Health Cooperative, in its effort to educate consumers and professionals about long-term care insurance, works with the insurance industry and regulators to improve the insurance products and constantly studies long term care policies. For current information on the best rates for long-term care insurance, contact United Seniors Health Cooperative, 1331 H Street, N.W., Suite 500, Washington, D.C. 20005, or call at 1-202-393-6222.

Long-term care insurance pays a fixed amount for each qualified day that your parent receives long-term care, either in a nursing home or at home. Policies continue to pay the benefit for a specific period, usually several years. Without insurance, your parent will pay the staggering cost of long-term care from his income and savings. After savings are depleted, this care is paid by Medicaid.

The premiums for long-term care increase with the age at which the policy is bought. The same policy might cost $1,800 per year for a sixty-five-year-old person, $2,500 for a seventy-year-old, and $4,400 for a seventy-five-year-old. For most Americans, these costs are prohibitive for modest or fixed incomes. A good rule of thumb is that your parent should have more than $40,000 in savings ($100,000 for a couple) before considering buying a long-term care insurance policy. Before he buys this policy, look at all of the ways available to protect his assets, and let this be another consideration in the total financial planning process.

MEDICAID

Medicaid provides long-term care for those elderly adults who qualify. To be eligible, the person must prove the need for nursing home care and meet certain income and asset levels. This federally funded, state-administered medical insurance program is for needy people.

The Medicaid program pays for medical care and related services. For adults, some services are limited by the number of times or the length of time the service can be continued or by the amount of money the program can pay. Call your district Medicaid office if you have any questions about service limitations. To preserve the parent's assets, planning must include an attorney with Medicaid experience if more than minimum assets are involved.

WHAT DOES MEDICAID COVER?

- Hospital services. Inpatient, outpatient, state mental hospitals, ambulatory surgical centers.

- Medical services. Services of doctors, advanced registered nurse practitioners (ARNP), chiropractors and podiatrists; prescribed drugs; certain medical supplies, appliances, and equipment; visual, hearing, laboratory, and x-ray services; community mental health services; and adult dentures.

- Medical services in special settings. Nursing home services, intermediate care facilities for the mentally retarded/developmentally disabled (ICF/DD), home health care, home and community based services, rural and federally qualified health centers (FQHC), HMOs, prepaid health plans, medipass, and hospice related services.

- Transportation to receive Medicaid services, and comprehensive assessment and review for long-term care services (CARES) evaluation.

Medicare and Medicaid. If your parent is eligible for Medicare and Medicaid, Medicare is considered the primary payer for services covered by Medicare. If your parent's provider accepts Medicare, he must accept assignment to Medicare and file the claim for your parent.

Check with your Social Security office to see what this program covers and to find out if this program would benefit your parent.

Medicaid Long-Term Care and Medicaid Gap. The term "working poor" describes many American citizens today. The working poor are those individuals who have worked for thirty years and raised a family on a low-salaried job. Their sparse life's savings, house, and meager pension usually qualifies these adults for *"Medicaid Gap."*

The "Medicaid Gap" candidate has too much income or too many assets to qualify for state Medicaid. Therefore, if illness or disability strikes a family of the working poor, long-term care, nursing home care, or group home care are all beyond the means of the family's ability to pay. The monthly cost of a nursing home now ranges from $2,500 upward per month depending on the quality of the facility and the area of the country.

One case involving an eighty-one-year-old man, William, is typical of people in this income category. This gentleman has no assets and lives on a meager pension of $1,446 per month from his railroad retirement. When he was recently diagnosed with Alzheimer's disease, his children found that his pension would only pay for half of his required nursing home care. Because William is unable to pay the difference, he is now faced with eviction from his home. William does not qualify for his state's Medicaid nursing home benefit because his income is $107 per month too much to qualify for Medicaid (his state allows benefits only if monthly income is below $1338). The problem is that there are too many cases just like William's where the senior is barely existing on a fixed income but makes a few dollars too much to receive state or federal assistance.

Medicaid Administered by the State

In planning for long-term care, inquire with your parent's state agency. The rules and limits as to assets and monthly income are determined by each state under federal guidelines and they vary state to state, just as the cost of living also varies.

AARP, welfare agencies, and county social workers can provide an individual with a copy of the rules.

Trust and Asset Transfers

The use of trust and asset transfers is a method that can be employed to qualify a person for Medicaid, but is governed by state statutes and the specific rules of the recipient's legal residence. Trusts can be complex documents and proper legal advice should be sought. A trust can either be revocable or irrevocable. As a rule, irrevocable transfer of assets and income producing assets are required before a person can be eligible for Medicaid. Each state has a maximum amount of assets an individual can retain. The formation of trusts and asset transfers must be done well in advance as each state has a "look back" provision (up to three years) and can disqualify one's eligibility for Medicaid if the transfers were made only for that purpose.

Property transfers usually by the elderly working poor are done for the purpose of giving their children a legacy. This is done usually with the giver's expectation.

Help for Low-Income Medicare Beneficiaries

If your parent has a low income and few resources, the state may pay his Medicare premiums and, sometimes, other "out-of-pocket" Medicare expenses such as deductibles and coinsurance. Only the state can decide if your parent qualifies.

Contact the state or local welfare office or the Medicaid agency. For more information about the program, contact your Social Security office and ask for the leaflet, *Medicare Savings for Qualified Beneficiaries* (HCFA publication No. 02184).

OTHER SERVICES

Supplemental Security Income. Supplemental Security Income or SSI is a program run by Social Security. SSI makes monthly payments to people who have low incomes and few assets. You should check to see if your parent's income falls into the category to qualify for SSI.

Food Stamps. Most seniors who get SSI can also get food stamps to help with food costs. For more information about food stamps, ask Social Security for a copy of the fact sheet, Food Stamp Facts (publication No. 05-10101).

Managing Benefits. Often people who receive Social Security or SSI are not able to handle their own financial affairs. In those cases, and after a careful investigation, the agency appoints a relative, a friend, or another interested party to handle the Social Security matters. That person is called a "representative payee." All Social Security or SSI benefits due are made payable in that representative payee's name on behalf of the beneficiary.

If you have a "power of attorney" for your parent, that does not automatically qualify you to be his or her representative payee. For more information, call Social Security and ask for a copy of the brochure entitled A Guide for Representative Payees (publication No. 05-10076).

When your parent creates a trust or transfer of property, these actions will have both income tax, gift tax, and estate tax consequences, and these tax problems are both on the federal and state level. *Irrevocable trusts* usually require the filing of annual tax returns. *Transfers of property* may require gift tax returns. You should contact your parent's tax advisors before any action is taken.

HOME EQUITY CONVERSION

Until recently there were only two ways your parent could get cash from his or her home: through a sale or a home equity loan if he qualified. In recent years, however, *home equity conversion plans* have become available in more areas of the country. The home equity conversion plan lets the adult turn the value of the home into cash without having to move or repay the loan each month. Based on the value of the equity, your parent would receive a fixed amount each month for a fixed number of years. The loan is repaid when the person moves or dies. AARP has a helpful booklet

Consumers Guide to Home Equity Conversion that offers useful information that will help you evaluate this option.

LOOK TO THE FUTURE FOR LONG-TERM CARE

Politicians are finally waking up to the crisis of long-term care in America. New legislation being considered daily affects this. These proposals are being closely monitored by watchdog groups such as the American Association of Retired Persons (AARP) to ensure that Medicare remains intact but with improvements for its beneficiaries.

MAKING A WINNING FINANCIAL PLAN

After you have considered the various options for long-term care, make a financial plan with your parent for the senior years that allows the assets to be kept intact.

TAKE AN INVENTORY

An inventory of all important details of financial affairs is the beginning step to making a financial plan. You will need to make at least three copies of this inventory, giving one copy along with other important papers to the executor, one copy to the attorney, and one copy for your parent. The inventory should include:

- A copy of the will. The executor should know where the original signed copy of the will is kept.

- A list of professionals, including names, addresses, and phone numbers. List the physician, pastor, attorney, accountant, insurance agent, financial planner, and others.

- A list of the safe deposit boxes, the bank box numbers, and the authorized signatures.

- A list of all bank accounts, account numbers, the type and key person, and authorized signatures.

- A list of insurance policies, including health, life, and any other policies with agents' names and phone numbers.

- An inventory of all investments.

- A list all debts (liabilities).

- A copy of financial statements.

DETERMINE YOUR PARENT'S NET WORTH

Once you start a financial inventory with your parent, recalculate this net worth on a regular basis, at least once a year. This shows the condensed value of the estate. The net worth will help to determine if the parent might qualify for any of the many federal and/or state programs, and it will show the assets and liabilities that will be used in the planning process.

Net Worth Form (Assets Owned Minus Liabilities Owed) Name_____Net Worth as of (Date)_____19__	
List all assets:	Amount
1. Cash (checking, money market etc.)	
2. CDs, US bonds, etc.	
3. IRAs, investments, etc.	
4. Stocks, bonds, including mutual funds	
5. Life insurance cash value	
6. Real estate investments (market value)	
7. Market value of home	
8. Other investments, assets	
9. Personal property (furniture, silver, jewelry, etc.)	
10. Other notes owed to parent, deposits, etc.	
11. Automobile(s) market value	
12. Total Assets (1 thru 11)	
List all liabilities:	Amount
13. Taxes due	
14. Monthly bills due (credit card, short-term debt)	

Net Worth Form (Continued) (Assets Owned Minus Liabilities Owed) Name_____Net Worth as of (Date)_____19__	
15. Remaining balance owed on mortgage(s)	
16. Balance owed on automobile(s)	
17. Other loans that you owe	
18. Liabilities (13 thru 17)	
19. Net Worth (12 minus 18) (value of parent's estate)	

ESTABLISH AN ATTAINABLE BUDGET

The budget is an important tool for everyone, but this financial plan of income and expenditures is especially helpful for those who live on fixed incomes. And the best place to begin outlining a budget with your parent is to start with the checkbook.

Go through the past three months with your parent and get an average of the monthly income and expenses from the checkbook.

For example, your parent may have a total of $2,500 per month in income and a total of $1,800 per month in regular expenses. List those items that are one-time only, biannual or annual (car repair, home owner's insurance, taxes, etc.). Determine this as a monthly average, and write down on the form. Once your parent understands how much money is coming in and where the expenditures are, expenses can better controlled. Review each item line by line and talk about ways to control unnecessary spending with your parent.

Consider the following categories in planning a retirement budget:

- *Housing.* You may want to consider the sale of the home and whether to seek smaller quarters, possibly a retirement facility, an apartment, or a smaller home. There are many benefits for seniors who wish to sell a home. It could possibly free up some cash for living expenses, medical bills, or investment purposes and could reduce the time-consuming upkeep and cost to maintain the home and yard. If your parent decides to sell the home, he may be able to take the one time exclusion of any accumulated gain on the sale of the home up to $125,000 for people over fifty-five years of age. If the home sale is a possibility, review it carefully with the financial and tax planner before the sale. If he decides to remain in the present home, be sure to have the utility company do an energy audit of the home for reducing the electric bill, and do a home safety check to see if any major home maintenance is needed.

- *Food.* Calculate the monthly food bill and see if costs could be cut by using coupons or joining a food co-op or warehouse plan.

- *Transportation.* Do your parents drive two cars? Can they cut back to one? This will help them realize a reduction in car payments, maintenance, insurance, and taxes.

- *Insurance.* Work with your parent's insurance agent and look for cost- effective coverage that provides security but perhaps has a higher deductible.

- *Medical and dental—out of pocket.* We have covered the preferred methods of paying for medical care, but your parent will have to pay some costs. Make sure this is well thought out with the options such as HMOs, Medigap, and long-term insurance considered.

- *Loans and credit cards.* If your parent is on a fixed income, discuss the hazards of using credit cards or taking out loans that may be a financial burden.

- *Clothing, recreation, and miscellaneous expenses.* Many expenses might not seem important but are necessary to budget to keep up your parent's self-esteem. New clothing will be needed during senior years and so will avenues for socialization. Encourage your parent to use senior citizens' discounts when possible.

- *Taxes.* At this stage in life, and especially if your parent is on a small, fixed income, taxes should be minimal. But it still is important to add this estimated amount into the budget to ensure it is covered.

Use the following personal expense form to calculate your parent's budget.

Personal Income and Expense Form
(monthly estimate)

EXPENSES	CURRENT YEAR
1. Housing, mortgage, taxes, utilities (electricity, water, gas & oil)	
2. Food, including home entertainment	
3. Transportation, payments, repairs	
4. Clothing and linens	
5. Insurance, including property, auto health & life	
6. Medical & dental—out of pocket	
7. Contributions & gifts	
8. Repayment of loans, credit cards, etc.	
9. Recreation—entertainment, vacations, sports events, hobbies, etc.	
10. Miscellaneous expenses	
11. Savings & retirement IRAs, company plan, investments, other	
12. Taxes (local, state, federal)	
13. Total expenses per month	
14. Total income this month	

Compare total expenses with the total income and make adjustments as indicated.

ESTABLISH A WILL

Whatever the size of the estate, your parent should have a will. The will is a legal document that distributes your parent's assets after death and names the executor of the estate.

A will must have two "disinterested" persons sign as witnesses. A handwritten will may be valid in a few states, but this is not recommended for it may be confusing, and the will could be thrown out.

Some states allow a form with "fill in the blanks" called a "statutory will." Those with smaller estates can take advantage of this type of will, but, again, any errors can invalidate the will. We recommend that you contact a lawyer to draw up a will for your parent to ensure it standing up in court. This will should be reviewed on a regular basis and promptly if your parent moves to a different state.

After you inventory your parent's net worth, list the assets and liabilities, and take inventory of important people and services. Meet with the estate planner and/or lawyer to draw up the will and formalize the estate plan.

ESTABLISH POWER OF ATTORNEY

General Power of Attorney. A general power of attorney is a document under which a person authorizes another person to act on his or her behalf. A special power of attorney is a document under which a person authorizes someone else to act on his behalf in specific situations only. The person who takes on the duty of power of attorney does not have to be a lawyer.

Health Care Power of Attorney. This document allows your parent to appoint an individual to make health care decisions if he or she should become incompetent, unconscious, or unable to make such decisions. This appointed person should be an adult whom he trusts and the following usually cannot be appointed: health-care providers, physician, employee of a hospital, nursing home, or residential home care facility unless the employee is related to your parent.

It is best for your parent to make his or her wishes known to the appointed person regarding the care and treatment. He might express wishes as to the following:

- Life sustaining procedures that would only delay the moment of death.

- Withdrawal or withholding of artificially administered nutrition and hydration.

- Procedures desired or not desired, access to medical records, authority to perform autopsy, or even desires as to continued care in a nursing home setting.

- Decision to take all measures that may sustain life rather than withdrawing or withholding such procedures.

Most health care providers should be able to guide you and your parent to documents that meet the state's requirements. The attorney should also assist in preparing this document, if needed.

LIFE INSURANCE IN SENIOR YEARS

When your parent begins to live off Social Security, pension, and savings, she should review her life insurance coverage. The coverage is not as important as it was when it would provide funds should the wage earner die. Have your parent meet with the financial planner to see if it makes sense to reduce or terminate some or even all of the coverage and have the premium dollars to spend on other things. If he decides to terminate a cash value policy, he can retrieve the accumulated funds. Some of the cash value may be taxable. Get financial and insurance advice before making any changes to the coverage.

AVAILABLE SUPPORT SERVICES

This information may seem confusing to many if you are just starting to understand the finances of aging. If you seek guidance from government agencies, professionals, and senior advocates such as your Area Agency on Aging, however, you will find the best possible answers to your parent's financial questions.

Review appendix B and call or write to the help agencies listed. Organizations such as AARP provide brochures that outline medical and financial benefits for seniors and how to apply for these. What is most important to remember is not to delay in seeking information and programs for your parent. Plan ahead financially with your parent to prevent undue crisis and to make for more secure senior years.

11

QUESTIONS CAREGIVERS ASK

Communication with the many professionals listed in chapter 3 is vital for compassionate caregiving that does not make you feel "all sandwiched in." After reading this book, write down any questions you or your parent may have before your next appointments, to ensure all questions will be addressed.

Here are the answers to commonly asked caregiving questions.

HOME ALONE

Q. My eighty-two-year-old father is frail but healthy. He refuses to come live with me or my brother, but we are worried that he might fall or become ill and no one will be there to help him. We both live more than an hour away from him. What should we do?

A. If your father needs to have supervision but wants to stay in his home, consider hiring a live-in companion. This would solve the problem of being "home alone," and give you some peace of mind. If this is not possible or affordable, consider home-sharing as discussed in chapter 5. You could also try an emergency response system. There are many viable alternatives you should check before moving an elderly parent out of his home, and you should exhaust all of these before considering a move.

Living with Arthritis

Q. My father has chronic pain from arthritis and has virtually given up. When I go to visit, he just sits in his chair and tells me how much he cannot do because of the pain. I almost hate to visit because I don't know what to do. How can I help?

A. Suggest that your father have a physical examination to rule out any other problems. If he is suffering from arthritis, ask his physician for a pain management program. Millions of seniors have arthritis and live an active life by managing pain. Many books on the market address the pain of arthritis and teach persons how to manage this without stopping living, including using an exercise program. Organizations such as the Arthritis Foundation and the American Chronic Pain Association can offer additional help (see app. B). Positive ways exist to attack pain and add active, happy years to your father's life.

Lonely Parents

Q. My father died two years ago, and my seventy-one-year-old mother is now in a rut. She is so bright and quite healthy, but she stays at home every day waiting for me or her neighbor to call or visit. What can I suggest so she will begin to take some initiative and develop a life of her own?

A. Review the exercise and activity chapter in this book, and then talk with your mother about the importance of getting out and being around people—other than family! She may enjoy helping at her church or volunteering with learning disabled children at a local elementary school. Perhaps she can recruit a new neighbor to walk with her each morning for exercise. Are there classes available at a recreation center or through adult education in the public schools? Whatever her interests are, talk with her about engaging in these to stay mentally stimulated and physically active. Have her write down in a notebook what she does each day, including things she has learned, people she talked with, or places she went to. Talk with her about these activities at the end of the week, and challenge her to make new discoveries in life. Be there for her, but don't let her life revolve totally around you. That is not fair for either of you.

COMMUNICATION DISORDERS

Q. I'm confused as to the various disorders that could cause speech and language problems. My father had a stroke several years ago and was recently diagnosed with dementia. He has a most difficult time communicating. Where do I turn for help?

A. Besides stroke, loss of language in elderly adults may also be due to brain tumors or other head injuries. Language loss is also associated with many neurological diseases typically found in the older population. A general term used to describe some of the progressive deterioration of the nervous system in the aged is dementia. Alzheimer's disease, for example, is a form of dementia.

If you would like to seek help for your father's communication disorder, ask his physician to recommend a speech-language pathologist for an evaluation. Make sure this person is a state licensed and nationally certified speech-language pathologist. You can contact the American Speech-Language-Hearing Association National Office at 1-301-897-5700 for more information.

FRAIL ELDERLY

Q. My ninety-two-year-old mother is very frail. She has the habit of rushing to answer the phone as soon as it rings. I'm afraid that she is going to fall. What can I do?

A. Many frail elderly have the same problem when they try to move too fast. Your mother probably looks forward to the phone conversation as part of her life. Call her at a certain time each day and tell her you will allow the phone to ring until she answers it (or at least ten times). Encourage her to call you if she feels that she missed your call. You can also have the phone company install a special feature that will allow her to call back the last person who

called her. This is an important feature for those who cannot get
to the phone in time.

Acting Your Age

*Q. My father is almost eighty-four years old, and he refuses to slow down
and act his age. I live in fear that he is going to get in an accident because
he still drives in rush hour traffic or that he is going to fall down the steep
stairs in his backyard. What can I do?*

A. Be thankful that your father can "act his age." Whatever he
feels like doing that is safe should be encouraged and applauded.
Think of the many seniors who would love to walk stairs but cannot due to physical weakness or the ones who would love to drive
but must sit at home due to physical problems.

There is a wonderful story told about a sixty-nine-year-old ethics
professor at a mid-western university who became ill with a debilitating neurological disease. When it became difficult to walk, he
used a cane to get to his classes. As the disease progressed, he went
to work each day in a wheelchair. In the final stages, he lost his
ability to talk, but he remained involved with his career by doing
research and even used a computer that selected words by the
movement of his eyes. While the disease took away his bodily functions, he never lost his determination and dignity.

Chances are that your father is an outstanding role model for
the elderly and helps to dispel the myth that old age means mental
and physical deterioration at a certain age. Encourage and praise
him as he lives with determination and dignity!

Project S.H.A.R.E.

*Q. I have heard about an organization that enables seniors to exchange
services for food. Have you heard of such?*

A. A Self Help and Resource Exchange (S.H.A.R.E.), located
throughout the country, is open to anyone who qualifies, regardless of income. Participants exchange a small amount of money
for food along with two hours of volunteer service each month for
a food package worth $25 to $35. The typical SHARE package con-
tains frozen meats, fresh fruits, vegetables, and dry food.

The volunteer service may be helping one's neighbor, church, school, or hospital. SHARE is not dependent upon government aid, and it is not a charity. It is self-supporting and funded by the people participating in the program. If the person wants more than one package, all he needs to do is double or triple the amount of money and volunteer hours he serves.

Many churches are involved in SHARE by becoming a SHARE host. Volunteers work hours by teaching Sunday School or Bible studies, helping in the church office, tending to children in the nursery, and more. Volunteers can also baby-sit for friends, care for a disabled friend or relative, help teachers in a school class-room, and do yardwork for a disabled person to get SHARE credit of at least two hours a month in helping others.

For more information on this program, call 1-800-726-7427.

SEEKING RESPITE CARE

Q. I live alone and take care of my ninety-year-old mother. Everyone tells me that I need to have respite care. Where do I look for this assistance?

A. Respite care means planned relief from your responsibilities as a caregiver. You can talk with friends and family members to or-ganize respite care and set up a schedule of relief. Check with your pastor and ask if church members would help fill in the gaps. If you still need resources, call your Area Agency on Aging and ask if your parent qualifies for services. You could hire someone through the newspaper or check with your local university's de-partments of social work, nursing, or geriatrics for names.

A HEALTHFUL DIET

Q. My mother is always sick, and the doctor said that she needs to eat a healthier diet to boost her immune system. I want to help her but do not know how.

A. A nutritional diet is critical for everyone's health. Ask her physician to recommend a registered dietician who could advise you and your mother about proper nutrition for the elderly. Re-read chapter 8 and talk about the importance of healthful foods with your mother. The National Council on Aging has an innovative forty-eight-page booklet entitled "Eat Well to Stay Well" that can give you an educational boost with creative ideas for planning healthful meals with her. Call toll free at 1-800-867-2755 for details on ordering. Ask for #4181 at $2.95, plus shipping.

YOUTH IN ACTION

Q. I am the youth director at a large church, and my youth would like to start a service project on assisting homebound elderly. How do we begin?

A. With your caring and dedicated Christian leadership, you are halfway there! Call the National Council on Aging at 1-800-867-2755 to order a book entitled *Let Us Serve Them All Their Days: Young Volunteers Serving Homebound Elderly Persons and a Handbook of Program Ideas.* The cost for this 170-page book is $15. Ask for #2051.

THE COSTS OF ALZHEIMER'S

Q. I read an article on Alzheimer's disease last week in a health magazine. My dad was just diagnosed, and the emotional and financial drain I read about frightens me to death. What should I do to prevent disaster?

A. This is a good time to arm yourself with the facts. Alzheimer's disease affects around 1.6 million Americans, and the latest reports say that the average cost for an Alzheimer's patient is from $20,000 per year for in-home care to $40,000 for a nursing home. The cost between diagnosis and death for the family is estimated to be more than $210,000. Check with the Area Agency on Aging and see if there are Alzheimer's support groups in your city. The more you can learn about the disease now, the better you will be able to prevent financial disaster. You can also call ADEAR (Alzheimer's Disease Education and Referral Center) at 1-800-438-4380.

VA SERVICES FOR THE ELDERLY

Q. My father is a veteran and is in need of long-term care. Does the VA provide these services?

A. Some VA medical centers provide nursing home care and private facilities for qualified individuals. Some facilities also provide domiciliary care (in VA facilities), personal care (in residential care homes), hospital-based home care, and in some states, family members are eligible for VA services. Contact your local VA office for details.

HOSPICE CARE FOR THE TERMINALLY ILL

Q. I have been taking care of my sixty-seven-year-old father who has cancer. His disease is progressing, and he wants to stay with us at home as long as possible. Can hospice help us?

A. Hospice is an agency that can provide comfort for terminally ill patients and their families in the home. Talk with his physician about using hospice and then contact the hospice in your area or have his doctor make this contact. Your father sounds as if he would qualify. He would greatly benefit from their services as would your entire family.

THE PERILS OF INCONTINENCE

Q. My parent has become homebound due to incontinence. How can we help him?

A. There are a number of ways to help this problem, both surgical and nonsurgical. Ask your father's physician to discuss the possible solutions with him. Be supportive and do not add to his embarrassment. Review chapter 2 on incontinence. Several agencies with support literature are listed in appendix B.

ELDER ABUSE

Q. I think an elderly woman in our neighborhood is being abused by her son. I hear her crying at night, and when I saw her at the grocery, she had bruises on her arms. I am not sure what to do, but I feel strongly about getting help.

A. You can call the Elder Abuse Hotline in your community to talk with a trained professional who will provide you with information on elder abuse and tell you how to seek assistance in your area. Abuse may include physical, mental, and emotional maltreatment in the care of a person (food, shelter, etc.) as well as self-maltreatment, meaning the person lives alone and cannot take care of himself. If you do have a strong suspicion, let someone know before it is too late.

SEEKING PROFESSIONAL GUIDANCE

Q. My eighty-nine-year-old father has taken a turn for the worse lately, but it is not something that I can put my finger on. He seems weaker, more withdrawn, and cries easily. What should I do?

A. Your father needs to make an appointment with his physician for a physical evaluation. Go with him and let the physician know about his diet, fluid intake, sleep and exercise habits, and bring his medications for review. Mention his withdrawal and frequent crying to the doctor as he checks out his mental health too, and then seek answers to the decline in your parent.

A CAREGIVER'S PROMISE

Q. Several years ago when my eighty-two-year-old mother first became ill, she asked me to promise never to put her in a nursing home. I gave her my word, but now she needs round-the-clock nursing care. I am exhausted, and I noticed that my two teens feel sad all the time as our home must be quiet in the evening hours. What should I do?

A. There comes a time when some promises made years before cannot always be kept, especially when it concerns the health and safety of an elderly person. Have a family meeting with siblings and talk about the caregiving dilemma and then delicately tell your mother the family's decision. If you are going to have to place her in a nursing home, try to get her input as to where she may want to live. You can make the commitment to visit her frequently while she is receiving the proper medical attention she needs. Remember the phrase "good enough." You can give so much, but you still must consider your life and the well-being of your family.

Seeking Home Care

Q. My elderly brother became homebound six months ago, and his wife was his caretaker. Now his wife is ill and must go to a nursing home. My brother is begging me to let him come live with my family. I want to care for my brother, but I have osteoporosis and am not sure I am strong enough to help him with physical tasks.

A. Is there any way you can hire a companion for him, or does he have room in his house to rent a room in exchange for physical assistance? If your brother is of sound mind, you can explore many avenues to allow him to live at home while still receiving the attention and help he needs. You must also protect your health. If both of you need assistance, that will help no one!

Deafness and the Elderly

Q. My seventy-year-old mother is partially deaf and has a most difficult time hearing the doorbell, the telephone, or even a car horn. I feel like a hearing aid might help, but she insists that she does not have a problem. How can I convince her to have her hearing checked?

A. Talk with her physician about the problem at her next visit. Could he suggest a hearing test as part of her physical exam? Often we all will listen to someone else, especially a "professional," when we ignore family members.

A Patient's Rights

Q. We are in the midst of a family quarrel. Our ninety-one-year-old mother has terminal cancer and the doctor gives her one year to live. She has accepted this and told us that she does not want heroic measures to save her life. My younger sister insists her doctors should do all they can to keep her alive. How can we convince our sister to adhere to Mother's wishes?

A. Have a family meeting with her physician or pastor (or both). Talk about your mother's situation and her personal wishes. Remember, this is her body, and you should honor what she wants to live with. Perhaps your sister has not accepted the reality of her mother's death and needs counseling to talk about this.

Has your mother made her wishes known either in writing or verbally? An "advanced directive" means a witnessed written document or oral statement in which instructions are given by a person or in which the person's desires are expressed concerning any aspect of health care and includes the designation of a health care surrogate, a living will, or a do-not-resuscitate order. She can do this through a "living will" or "declaration," which is a witnessed legal document in which the signer voluntary requests not to be kept alive by medical life-support systems in the event of a terminal illness. This can also be a witnessed oral statement expressing the person's instructions concerning life-prolonging procedures.

Living wills grew out of conflicts between physicians and families about which treatments could be discontinued when there was no hope of recovery for the patient. Your mother's desires about treatment, such as refusing forced feedings or liquids, surgery, and medications can be put into this living will. You will definitely want to seek the advice of an attorney if you want to prepare this with her.

DRIVING AND THE ELDERLY

Q. My eighty-six-year-old mother still drives and has had three small wrecks in the last year. I am a nervous wreck thinking about her being on the highway. How can we talk her into giving up driving without losing her pride?

A. Be honest with your mother. Tell her you are concerned for her safety and for others. Tell her you will assist in getting transportation and follow through with commitments from family and friends. Other organizations can help with transportation including church members, the Red Cross, and senior organizations in the community.

TELLING CHILDREN ABOUT ILLNESS

Q. We just found out that our father has Alzheimer's disease. He has been so close with our children, and we do not know how to tell them. How long should we act like things are normal, or must we tell them that Granddaddy is very sick?

A. Realize that you cannot hide Alzheimer's disease. Talk to your children about the disease using age-appropriate terms, but without going into details. Explain to them the progression of the disease so they can be compassionate when Granddaddy acts "different," but do so in a manner that does not frighten them. And let your children be around your parent—Alzheimer's patients need love and care as much as anyone else in this world.

You can have your pastors meet with your family, or if a social worker is assisting your father, she can refer you to trained professionals who can talk with your children.

EATING ALONE

Q. My mother hates to eat alone, so many times she just snacks on food instead of having a balanced meal. We invite her over three times a week to join our family, but she needs answers for the other days. What should she do?

A. Eating alone can seem depressing for many mature adults, but they can take steps to remedy this. Urge her to invite friends over to join her for meals during the week. Each friend can bring a favorite dish, and they can enjoy the company and new foods. Buy her a new tablecloth and basket of flowers to put on her table. She can set the table each night with her favorite china, turn on some music, and change the atmosphere of the home to be more conducive for dining. She can also go out with friends to eat in restaurants. Many reasonably priced restaurants offer early supper menus for seniors at reduced costs.

THE BENEFITS OF PETS

Q. My mother lives alone and has an active life with many friends. We were thinking about getting her a dog for company and for some protection. Is this a good idea?

A. Pets can be wonderful for people of all ages. Some studies have shown that people who have pets also have lower blood pressure. A dog can give your mother much-needed companionship as well as protection against intruders. Make sure the breed you choose is easy for your parent to handle.

Wheelchair Bound

Q. My father is confined to a wheelchair, but he used to be so active. Where do we look for ideas on getting him involved in activities?

A. Several national organizations can refer you to groups in your city for wheelchair-bound seniors. You can call or write to the National Handicapped Sports and Recreation Association or the Disabled Sportsman. Both addresses are listed in appendix B.

Ask your father's physician to recommend a physical therapist who can show your father strengthening exercises. It will certainly increase his feeling of well-being if he has an outlet. Exercises can help decrease his stiffness and maintain and improve his mobility. He could possibly benefit from weight training, isometrics, and isotonic exercises.

One Senior's Secret

Q. Is there a secret to a happy, long life? Since my mother died, my seventy-one-year-old father mopes around his house all day. I know he is bored. He is so healthy and could be enjoying his life. What should I do?

A. One of the most healthy, active, and well-adjusted women we've ever seen is a Christian woman named Caroline. We asked Caroline to give us her secret to happiness, and she wrote:

> I believe in enjoying life to the fullest. I've always worked hard, even two jobs sometimes. I believe in serving God and respecting other people. I was very active before I retired, but I'm still involved with many activities in the community and at my church. I think it pays to stay active; it helps keep me young and healthy. Of course, rest is important, too. I eat a lot of vegetables, stay away from fried foods and salt, and rarely eat sweets. I don't smoke or drink. At seventy-six years old, I have been a widow twice, but my life is filled with a love for God, my church, and others. I thank God every day for blessing me with good health and an active retirement.

Now, doesn't that say it all?

APPENDIX A:
SELECTING A PROFESSIONAL—
SAMPLE INTERVIEW

Name: Date:
Address: Phone:

QUESTIONS FOR THE PROFESSIONAL

1. What type of training do you have?

2. When and where did you graduate from school? What other
    training do you have?

3. Are you board certified (if physician) or do you have re-
    quired certifications of the governing agency?

4. What is your hospital affiliation (if this is a health care profes-
    sional)?

5. Can you be reached by telephone twenty-four-hours a day?
    Do you have an emergency number?

6. Who covers for you when you are away?

7. What experience do you have working with elderly clients or patients?

8. Do you charge a reasonable rate? Do you accept assignment, agreeing to accept whatever Medicare pays and not bill for the difference? (Can your parents afford this or will Medicare, private insurance company, or a federal agency pay for this?)

Other Information:

9. Ask for references of other clients and interview them about their experiences working with this professional.

10. Does the professional treat you and your parent with respect?

11. Do you and your parent trust this person?

APPENDIX B:
SENIOR ADVOCATE GROUPS AND RESOURCES

There is a vast amount of information on aging, including special services your parent may need—if you know where to look. In this appendix you can broaden your knowledge of aging as you seek local and national help for your parent.

COMMON LISTINGS IN THE TELEPHONE BOOK

It is often difficult to find the telephone number for an organization if you are unsure of the proper name. The following list gives the most common listings for aging services.

Adult abuse registry

Adult congregate living facilities

Adult day care

Aging services

Area Agency on Aging

Arthritis Foundation

Assisted living facility

Better Business Bureau

Board and care homes

Cancer Society

Convalescent services

Crisis hotline

Churches

ECHO housing

Family service agency

Fire department

Geriatric care managers

Handicapped services, transportation, equipment

Health department

Health and rehabilitation services (HRS)

Home health care

Hospice

Internal Revenue Service

Library

Long-term care

Meals on Wheels

Medicaid

Medicare

Mental Health Association

National Council on Aging

National Health Information Center

Nursing home

Occupational therapy

Physical therapy

Poison control

Police department

Postal services

Public health department

Public utilities

Recreation centers

Red Cross

Senior citizen services, organizations

Senior services

Social Security

Social worker

Speech therapy

Subsidized housing

Suicide crisis center

Veteran's Administration

Visiting Nurses' Association

Volunteer organizations

YMCA/YWCA

HUMAN SERVICES

Check the front of the yellow pages under Human Services for a listing of available services, addresses, and phone numbers, many of which are specifically for senior citizens.

Abuse

Alcohol and drug abuse

Burns

Consumer assistance

Counseling and mental health

Crisis intervention

Day care

Emergency preparedness

Employment

Financial and food assistance

Handicapped services

Health information

Housing assistance

Housing emergency

Legal services

Medical and dental services

Recreation facilities

Senior citizens' services

Support groups

Transportation

Volunteer opportunities

Toll-Free Numbers
for Senior Support Organizations

Toll free numbers often give access to resources that are not available in your community. You can also dial 1-800-555-1212 (directory assistance for national toll free numbers), if you know the name of the organization or if a number has been changed or disconnected.

Alzheimer's Association 1-800-272-3900

Alzheimer's Disease Education and Referral Center (ADEAR Center) 1-800-438-4380

American Foundation for the Blind 1-800-829-0500

American Association of Kidney Patients 1-800-749-2257

American Diabetes Association 1-800-232-3472

American Lung Association 1-800-LUNG -USA

American Parkinson Disease Association 1-800-223-2732

American Physical Therapy Association 1-800-999-2782

American Speech-Language-Hearing Association 1-800-638-8255

Arthritis Foundation 1-800-283-7800

Cancer Information Service 1-800-422-6237

Elder Care Locator 1-800-677-1116

Enrichment Inc. 1-800-323-5547

Grief Recovery Helpline 1-800-445-4808

Help for Incontinent People 1-800-BLADDER

Home Health Aid Catalog 1-800-321-0595

Medicare "B" Claims (Call 1-800-555-1212 and ask for the agency for your state)

National Council on Aging (NCOA) 1-800-867-2755

National Stroke Association 1-800-787-6537

Sear's Home Health Care Catalog 1-800-948-8800 (Ask for the Home Health Care Catalog—free of charge)

The Simon Foundation for Continence 1-800-23SIMON

Social Security 1-800-772-1213

Senior Advocates

At this printing, the following agencies and addresses respond promptly to queries for information.

AARP

American Association of Retired Persons

601 E. Street, N.W.

Washington, DC 20049

(If you write to the Research Information Group, c/o AARP, you will receive an order form listing available brochures. Allow four to six weeks. This organization should be able to point you in the right direction on almost any issue dealing with aging, as well as offer numerous booklets on aging.)

Academy for Elder Law Attorneys
655 N. Alvernon Way
Alvernon Place (Suite 108)
Tucson, AZ 85711
(Request "Questions and Answers when Looking for an Elder Law Attorney.")

Advil Forum on Healthcare
1500 Broadway, 26th Floor
New York, NY 10036
(Ask for brochure on pain relief for osteoporosis, back pain, arthritis, and more.)

"Age Pages," Consumer Information Center
P. O. Box 100
Pueblo, CO 81002
(The catalog is free; "Age Pages" will have a fee.)

Aids for Arthritis
3 Little Knoll Court
Medford, NJ 08055
1-609-654-6918

Alzheimer's Association
919 N. Michigan Ave., Suite 1000
Chicago, IL 60611
1-800-272-3900
(Call for information on caregiving.)

Alzheimer's Disease Education and Referral Center (ADEAR)
P.O. Box 8250
Silver Springs, MD 20907-8250
1-800-438-4380
(Call or write for information on Alzheimer's Disease.)

American Association of Homes and Services for the Aging
901 E. St. N.W., Suite 500
Washington, DC 20004-2037
1-202-783-2242

American Association of Kidney Patients
100 S. Ashley Drive, Suite 280
Tampa, FL 33602
1-800-749-2257

American Cancer Society
1599 Clifton Rd., N.E.
Atlanta, GA 30329
1-800-ACS -2345

American Chronic Pain Association
P. O. Box 850
Rocklin, CA 95677
1-916-632-0922

American Diabetes Association
1660 Duke St.
P. O. Box 25757
Alexandria, VA 22314
1-800-232-3472

American Heart Association
7272 Greenville Ave.
Dallas, TX 75231-4596
1-214-373-6300

American Lung Association
432 Park Ave., S.
New York, NY 10016
1-800-LUNG-USA

American Parkinson Disease Association
60 Bay St., Suite 401
Staten Island, NY 10301
1-800-223-2732

American Speech-Language-Hearing Association National Office
10801 Rockville Pike
Rockville, MD 20852
1-301-897-5700; Fax 1-301-571-0457

Area Agency on Aging or the Administration on Aging
U.S. Department of Health and Human Services
Dept. BHG
Independence Avenue, SW
Washington, DC 20201

Arthritis Foundation
1314 Spring Street, N.W.
Atlanta, GA 30309
1-800-283-7800

Assisted Living Facilities Association of America
Dept. BHG
10322 Blake Lane
Oakton, VA 22124

Canine Companions for Independence
P. O. Box 446
Santa Rosa, CA 95402-0446
1-707-528-0830

Children of Aging Parents
Woodbourne Office Campus, Suite 302-A
1609 Woodbourne Road
Levittown, PA 19057
(Send $1.00 and SASE for information and referral.)

Christian Record Services, Inc.
4444 S. 52nd St.,
Lincoln, NE 68516
1-402-488-0981
(Write or call for information on records and large print magazines for the visually impaired.)

Christian Tapes for Disabled
P. O. Box 455
Buffalo, NY 14209

Corporate Angel Network
Westchester County Airport
Building One
White Plains, N. Y. 10604
(Write for a listing of private corporations that assist cancer patients who are in need of air transportation.)

Christmas in April
1225 Eye St.
Washington, DC 20005
1-202-326-8268
(Write for information on home repair for low income elderly. This organization will assist groups such as churches and nonprofit agencies in starting a program entitled "Christmas in April" in your area.)

Clearinghouse of Disability
U.S. Dept. of Education
Office of Special Education and Rehab. Services
Switzer Building, Room 3132
Washington, DC 20202-2524
1-202-708-5366

(Write for a summary of existing legislation for disabilities, and pocket guide to help individuals with disabilities.)

Cleo, Inc.
3958 Mayfield Road
Cleveland, OH 44121
1-800-321-0595
(Write for information on medical equipment and products used for patient rehabilitation. Ask for catalog.)

Consumer Information Center
S. James
P. O. Box 100
Pueblo, CO 81002
1-719-948-9724
(Write or call for a catalog of pamphlets or brochures available on a variety of subjects.)

Disabled Sportsman
P. O. Box 5496
Roanoke, VA 24012

Elder Care Letter
P. O. Box 420423
Palm Coast, FL 32142-0123
(Write to order subscription to newsletter.)

Family Service America
11700 W. Lake Park Drive
Milwaukee, WI 53224

Foster Grandparent Program
Corporation for National Service
1100 Vermont Ave., N.W.
Washington, DC 20525
1-202-678-4215

Gray Panthers
3635 Chestnut St.
Philadelphia, PA 19104

Elizabeth Owens Haseman, Ph.D.C.C.C.
Speech-Language Pathologist
503 Fern Cliff Avenue
Temple Terrace, FL 33617
1-813-899-0421
(Write or call to purchase an inexpensive home workbook containing speech and language drills and activities.)

Help for Incontinent People
P. O. Box 544
Union, SC 29379

Hostelships
Elderhostel
80 Boylston St., Suite 400
Boston, MA 02116

Legal Council for the Elderly (LCE)
1009 K St., N.W.
Washington, DC 20049
1-202-434-2120

LSPN (Let's Stop Pain Now)
1-813-989-8409
(Call for brochure of current literature on the management of arthritis, back pain, osteoporosis, chronic pain, or heart attack.)

Managing Medications
Dept. S
P.O. Box 15329
Stamford, CT 06901
(Send a self-addressed stamped envelope for information on recognizing adverse drug reactions.)

Meals on Wheels
(Contact your local Area Agency on Aging and find out what organizations deliver food to senior citizens in your area.)

National Association for Home Care
519 C Street N.E, Station Park
Washington, DC 20002-5809

National Association of Area Agencies on Aging
1112 16th St. N.W.
Suite 100
Washington, DC 20036
(Check for the agency in your town or call 1-800-555-1212 to get the number of the nearest agency.)

National Association of Private Geriatric Care Managers
1604 N. Country Club Rd.
Tucson, AZ 85716
1-602-881-8008

National Consumers League
815 Fifteenth Street, NW
Suite 516
Washington, DC 20005
1-202-639-8140

National Council on the Aging, Inc.
Dept. 5087
Washington, DC 20061-5087
1-800-867-2755
(Write to order a catalog of publications.)

National Council of Senior Citizens
925 15th St. N.W.
Washington DC 20005
1-202-347-8800

National Guardianship Association
136 South Keowee Street
Dayton, OH 45402
1-513-222-1024

National Handicapped Sports and Recreation Association
1145 19th St., NW
Suite 717
Washington, DC 20036
1-301-652-7505

National Hispanic Council on Aging
2713 Ontario Rd., N.W.
Washington, DC 20009
1-202-265-1288

National Hospice Organization
1901 North Moore Street, Suite 901
Arlington, VA 22209

National Institute on Adult Day Care
NCOA Publications (Order #2050)
Dept. 5087
Washington, DC 20061-5087
(Write and ask for #2050 for information on adult day cares.)

National Institute on Aging Information Center
2209 Distribution Center
Silver Springs, MD 20910

National Osteoporosis Foundation
1150 17th St., N.W. Ste 500
Washington, DC 20036
1-202-223-2226

National Self-help Clearing House-CUNY
Graduate Center
33 W. 42nd St.
Room 1222
New York, NY 10036

National Senior Sports Association
10560 Main St.
Fairfax, VA 22030
1-703-758-8297

National Stroke Association
8480 E. Orchard Rd., Ste. 1000
Englewood, CO 80110
1-800-787-6537

Older Women's League
666 11th St. N.W.
Washington, DC 20001
1-202-783-6686

P.R.I.D.E. Foundation (Promote Real Independence for the Disabled and Elderly)
391 Long Hill Rd.
Box 1293
Groton, CT 06430
1-203-445-1448

Reach to Recovery
c/o American Cancer Society
1599 Clifton Road, N.E.
Atlanta, GA 30329
1-800-422-6237

Recordings for the Blind
20 Roszel Road
Princeton, NJ 08540
1-609-452-0606

Salvation Army
P. O. Box 269
Alexandria, VA 22313
1-703-684-5500

Simon Foundation for Continence
Box 815
Wilmette, IL 60091
1-800-23SIMON

Society for the Advancement of Travel for the Handicapped
347 5th Ave., Ste. 610
New York, NY 10016
1-212-447-7284

Telephone Preference Service
c/o Direct Mail Marketing Association
6 E. 43rd St.
New York, NY 10017
(Write for information on how to get off a phone list.)

Society for the Right to Die
250 W. 57th St.
New York, NY 10107
(For information on Living Wills and Durable Power of Attorney.)

Widowed Persons Service
c/o AARP
601 E. St., N.W.
Washington, DC 20049
1-202-434-2277

CALL FOR SUPPORT

The American Self-Help Clearinghouse will give information on caregiving support groups. Write or call:

American Self-Help Clearinghouse
St. Clares-Riverside Medical Center
Pocono Road
Denville, NJ 07834
1-201-625-7101